b

Banking and Currency

and

The Money Trust

By

CHARLES A. LINDBERGH

DEDICATED TO THE PUBLIC

NATIONAL CAPITAL PRESS, INC.
BOOK MANUFACTURERS
WASHINGTON, D. C.

2

The market prices of commodities vary from day to day and often several times a day. This occurs when there is no radical difference in the proportion of the supply and the natural demand. This fact is conclusive proof that our system is controlled by manipulators and fundamentally wrong. I have sought to elucidate this problem within this volume and have suggested a plan which, if adopted, would make the people the master of the world, instead of the present master—THE MONEY TRUST.

By Charles A. Lindbergh, Author of the Money Trust Investigation.

CONTENTS

	PAGE
GENERAL OBSERVATIONS	5
INTRODUCTION	8
IN CONTEMPLATION	15
WHAT IS THE MATTER WITH US?	26
CURRENCY, BANKING, AND THE MONEY TRUST	33
INTEREST, DIVIDENDS AND RENTS	138
SHORT SELLING	161
THE POLITICAL ASPECT OF THE PROBLEM OF FINANCES	168
GOVERNMENT GUARANTEE OF BANK DEPOSITS	177
MONEY	183
THE REMEDY	195
A TWO-FOLD REMEDY REQUIRED	220
THE PRACTICAL SIDE OF A BETTER FINANCIAL SYSTEM	272
APPENDIX A	289
APPENDIX B	299

The price of this book is $1, cloth bound,
50 cents, paper bound.

Copies may be secured from
C. A. LINDBERGH,
LITTLE FALLS,
MINNESOTA.

GENERAL OBSERVATIONS.

The material production and consumption by the people, and industries of the world go on continually. In the aggregate there is no perceptible difference from day to day, or even from month to month. All things considered, the proportion of supply and demand does not vary greatly from year to year. The catastrophies which occur in the world are usually confined to different localities at different times, and do not, on the whole, change the general result. Nature seems to keep the balance fairly well, at least well enough so that man need not fear that Nature will fail to respond to the needs of men.

We meet a different condition when we study the personal and commercial relations of the people with each other. When we do that we find an intensely variating condition, which works rapidly backward and forward with no or at least comparatively little, relation to the material conditions. These human conditions seem to have exhausted the patience of men and they are reaching out to make three great changes:

(A) A change in the banking and currency conditions;

(B) A readjustment of our industrial relations;

(C) A change in the political conditions so that the people as a whole may direct their own political affairs.

Bankers, merchants, professional men, farmers, and wage earners all know that a change in our banking and currency laws is imperative. Such a change is sure to come, and Wall Street is endeavoring to foster ideas in the public mind which will insure the adoption of a plan favorable to frenzied finance. Civilization has reached the point where the people ought to consider the following facts: That we are slaves of a money system; that market quotations fluctuate up and down at times when there is no corresponding change in the supply and natural demand; and that the Wall Street financiers have suddenly found time to leave their speculative schemes long enough to direct the work of educating the people in the mysteries of finance. Are these financiers working in the interests of the people or in their own interests? They were content to deal only with the boss politicians until the people themselves began taking an interest in legislation, but now that the people have admonished the bosses, Wall Street is trying to mould public opinion in order to make it favorable to some disguised Wall Street plan.

These questions are all answered in this little volume. Also, a plan is proposed which if adopted will make the people the master of the world and the builders of their common fortunes, instead of leaving that power in the clutches of its present master—the Money Trust.

We live in an age of mechanical devices and have the use of methods by which the natural elements are harnessed and made use of in general production, and in the establishment of conditions that serve to produce whatever is necessary, convenient and proper to the enjoyment of life, and it is natural that men shall look forward to the time when the people themselves will secure the full benefit of all these things. I have taken these problems up for consideration in three separate volumes. This volume on Banking and Currency and the Money Trust is the first. The second will be on "The Industrial Relations," and the third on "The Political Relations."

INTRODUCTION.

It would seem that one could not state and analyze so difficult a problem as that of banking and currency within the scope of a small volume, but I believe that it can be done and can be easily understood if properly treated. No civil matter that has arisen out of our present social condition was ever of greater importance than that which is contemplated as a basis of our first study, which is really the money problem. But this first study is only one of several that we shall make while investigating the highways and byways of business, politics, and those affairs of life which force men into the environments that are not of their own choosing. ¡We shall study conditions that are quite ordinary, and show their relations to others that are extraordinary and not generally understood. I have examined and know about the subjects to which we shall give our thoughts, and if a majority will join with me in these considerations, I am certain that within a very short time we shall all understand much more clearly the present conditions, and learn to make

8

the best use of the advantages that are common to all mankind. We shall also discover the reason for their being daily neglected. We shall not be able, in a short study, to cover the entire field, but it will present to us such things as are not commonly known to exist. Some of us have suspected that conditions exist about which we know very little or nothing, but the most of us have looked calmly on and decided eventually that there was something wrong. What is it? Our studies will tell.

The fact that I am a Congressman and seeking to force these matters before Congress for correction will cause me to be publicly censured for exposing the nature of the affairs of certain interests which have been prospering for a long time by appropriating the products of our toil. Numerous fires have been and will continue to be set under me by those who are selfishly interested in maintaining the present Money Trust, which not only includes many of the greatest bankers, but all others, in whatsoever business, who are beneficiaries of the system, as well as the political bosses subservient to the great interests. Of course they know that when the public once realizes how outrageously it has

been, and is being, fleeced it will not permit it
any longer, and they resort to desperate and
tricky methods in their attempt to force me out
of public office, because they realize that in my
present position I have an excellent opportunity
to direct public attention to the truth relating
to the practices of the banks and other special
interests.

It is a well-known fact that in forcing through
Congress the investigation of the Money Trust,
I laid bare one of their innermost secrets, even
though the investigating committee was composed of men selected by them after the interests were unable to prevent the passage of a
resolution to investigate. But regardless of
this fact, the environments surrounding the
committee's work forced out facts which will
aid in ultimately exposing the whole piratical
system. This seems to them to be the great
offense that I have committed, and therefore
they do all that they can to weaken me before
the public. Already, by means of their agents,
they have begun to spread stories. These
stories they wish the people to unwittingly ped-
dle from one to another. Underhandedly they
start one or more falsehoods in each locality

and hope that by the time these are peddled among my constituents enough of them will be believed to be true so that each voter shall find something to which he objects. In that way they hope that at least a majority of the voters can be secured who will vote against me. That is a scheme that is in operation, and for the same reason a certain portion of the press was subsidized to oppose me. Newspapers print scurrilous articles and others in the same employ copy them. Some articles are inserted which contain a few complimentary words about me for having done some unimportant thing, but these are diplomatically inserted in order to impress the reader with the idea that the editor is impartial. This impression is what they rely upon to give the color of truth to the opprobrious and derogatory matter.

My fight against graft in politics and special privileges in business has not resulted in my landing in a bed of roses. The public has seen that, and I knew from the start that I would have to fight every inch of the way as well as pay my own expenses, while those who opposed me, and consequently my plans, would have their campaign and other expenses paid, including other advantages which would be extended to them. I observe, for instance, that the stand-pat Senators and Representatives, all of whom are more or less under the domination of the special privileges, and stand-patters generally, have received recognitions and courtesies from the Administrations that have been absolutely refused to me. All sorts of dishonest and unfair means have been resorted to in order to injure me, while, on the other hand, every kind of deception has been used in the attempt to make the public believe that the Senators and Representatives who have supported the special interests were all right. This fight has not been easy nor has it been personally profitable to me from a financial standpoint. My purpose in calling attention to these facts is, that almost everyone who undertakes to establish reforms, that involve substantial property rights or personal privileges, receives the knocks and the least material reward. Further, the attacks made upon them by the special interests often mislead the public. That, of course, is the real purpose of the attacks, and every person must endure them who assails with vigor the system under which the special interests are able to levy tolls upon us for their maintenance.

Lest there might be some misunderstanding, I wish the real attitude of the bankers on this subject of the Money Trust to be known. Many of them, and more especially those from the country districts, are not opposed to reform. They know that they have special privileges that they ought not to have. In fact, the greatest number of them are opposed to the Money Trust. I have received letters from hundreds of them, but in nearly every instance they request that I keep secret the fact that they oppose the Money Trust. They dare not endanger themselves, and they do well not to as long as the present system is continued, for no bank would be safe if the Money Trust sought to close its doors.

I do not intend to arouse any distrust of your banker. He is a citizen the same as the rest of us. I am not assailing him, but I am assailing with all the vigor of my life the system of banking and currency that so taxes our existence, and I am seeking to prevent the Money Trust from fooling us into adopting changes that will allow it to retain its power. And I further seek to bring about a change that will enable us to retain the products of our own energy and give therefrom such moiety to those who render service as they may be entitled to by reason of their services.

We do not expect perfection either in ourselves or in others, but we should at least fulfill the plain necessities of life to the extent of not being ridiculous in our failures. For that reason there should be no delay in pressing the fight for our common rights and enforcing them through the intelligence of our conduct. We should not waive our individual rights in support of other's vanity, nor give them undeserved wealth or authority.

IN CONTEMPLATION.

To AMERICA: What a grand expanse of territory! Behold the majesty of her mountains; the vastness of her plains; her enormous forests; her wealth of soils and minerals; the number of her lakes; her splendid rivers leading to the natural highways between all lands and continents—the mighty oceans, and all—all of these are the free gifts of God to Man.

To MAN: Behold him in his application with the free gift—America. He has gone out over the plains and through the forests; developed the farms; built beautiful villages and great cities; constructed highways; furnished communication between them all; and then developed them by his ingenuity. All these are the expressions of his own energy—the results of his toil, but, notwithstanding the gifts of God and the giving by Man of his own energy, he is burdened with a huge debt—the greater because of the largeness and richness of Nature, the expenditure he has made of his energy, and the accumulation by the few of the products. Why should we all labor to produce material wealth

called capital, when it is appropriated by the
few and made the basis on which they tax us
and collect from us more interest and dividends?

To THE JOKER:

HERE I HOLD A GOLD COIN

What a false illusion thou art to human mind!
How cruelly thou deceivest thy possessor and
those who covet thee! Thou buyest for me by
thy betrayal of mankind. Thou didst tax my
energy to gain thee, and thy discount has lost
to me and my fellow-men the greatest blessings
of a continent, as well as the principal products
of our toil. Few indeed are they who know
and understand thy seductive power. We shall
expose thy falseness so that our children shalt
not be deceived by thee.

To OURSELVES: The fact that we did not prevent the various evils of which we now complain
from becoming parts of our system, should
make us considerate of those who are operating
under it, and remove from us all personal
prejudice. The practices that are allowed at
present, and which are contrary to what we
know to be for the best interests of mankind as

a body, are almost wholly due to the process of adaptation and not to the mere personal choice of some particular individuals.

Men are compelled to employ the methods and systems that are used in their times. No one can set up an independent system for himself and operate under it without the help and consent of the majority of his fellow-men. He must abide by, and operate under, the recognized systems regardless of the fact that neither the means nor the method may suit him. For that reason it is neither uncommon nor improper for us to do many things of which we do not ourselves approve. It is impossible for anyone to have a successful business career who does not conduct it in accordance with and in systematic concert with the prevailing methods, and therefore in the study and discussion of the affairs connected with the general conduct of business we should be broad in our interest, and honestly try to understand everybody, whether they conduct their business in the way that we think proper or not.

We should remember that we are dealing with systems and not with individuals, and that we have no right to blame individuals for the present system nor because they use it, but we have a right to ask them to examine it carefully, and if they find errors, to join in an endeavor to correct them and not make an unfair use of the opportunities such errors may present to them. Radical changes are not possible until they come by common consent.

Mankind is restless, and the broad field presented to the human intellect and selfishness, combined with the ambitious desire for prominence and leadership, impels it onward in a great and endless struggle. Individuals drop out as time advances, but humanity as a body presses onward. We inherit, fit into, adjust and renew the establishments and systems of our fathers, and what changes we do make are made through natural evolution, which is slow or rapid according to our inventive and creative energy and our acceptance, as a whole, of the change.

War has been one of mankind's greatest occupations, or, in other words, the exercise of government by the law of physical force. It has been esteemed a manly art, and all men have paid the toll, including the numerous toilers who provide provisions and munitions of war and supplement those in the actual field of combat.

It has been the mighty burden that the past has had to carry, and we still carry war obligations because the general understanding of this problem has not been sufficient to cause it to be absolutely abandoned. The comparatively few who have understood have had to fight the same as those who did not, somewhat on the same principle that we are forced to do business as business is done, or stop trying, which men will not do until they can no longer push as hard as they are pushed. But, even now, although we know that war is merely a legacy from the earlier generations, we realize that we cannot prevent it merely because we no longer think favorably of it. Civilization has advanced almost to the period of framing a plan for abandoning it, but all men and all peoples do not reach the same plane of understanding at the same time. We must still keep prepared for war because it is not improbable that we shall have some great wars long after we have finally concluded that war is an improper method to use for the settlement of disputes. So, too, in the world of business, some unsatisfactory, in fact bad, methods will continue, and it may be necessary for them to continue long after we know them to be neither just or desirable.

The great struggle of the present is centered in the world of commerce and trade. It has become so intense that the outlet for human ambition has shifted notably from the field of war to that of commercial struggle. In fact, the commercial struggle often produces the cause of war. This industrial struggle is another and much more humane diversion. I say diversion because whenever commerce is resorted to for speculation rather than for the purpose of supplying needs, it becomes a diversion. Some interesting comparisons may be drawn between the respective leaders and workers in these two fields of action, comparisons which may serve to make more clear the difference between the social and financial conditions of the governed and the governing.

History records the glorious achievements and victories gained by the military generals. But although it relates the honors and positions that were given the leaders as rewards for their initiative, it gives no specified individual record of the plain soldiers who fought the battles and suffered the privations and tortures incident to

war. These were considered as an army,—
merely the force with which the generals fought.
The great wizards of finance and the captains of
commercial industry also direct battles and
seek the same sort of acclamation growing out
of an entirely different application of human
energy and for another kind of victory. Their
wealth and their struggle repays them and its
buying and ruling properties win for them ap-
plause, position, and power.

It is probably easier to be a toiler in some
branch of commercial industry than to be a
soldier or sailor and direct the sword and can-
non against one's fellow-mortals, but the toilers,
the same as the soldiers, are the plain people.
On them depends the result of the struggle. On
them rests the greatest part of the work, the
denials and the sufferings, but contemporaneous
history makes no more individual recognition
of them than it did of the private soldier. Notwithstanding this seeming inconsistency, we
owe thanks to the financial wizards and the captains of industry for leading us out into the industrial field and away from that of war,
because it provides a better outlet for human
energy. It was the next move in the march of

civilization, and these captains of industry have been leaders in the struggles. Often it is the cruel and unreasonable who accomplish more for us than the kind and generous. They reveal to us our limitations. But there is no more reason to condemn the industrial generals than there has been to condemn the generals who fought in the world's great army and navy battles. The highest purpose of civilization should be to conserve and protect humanity, and whatever defeats that purpose should be condemned and eliminated.

No such destruction of human life can ever result from the industrial struggles as resulted from those of armed battle. The element of construction is far greater than that of destruction, and regardless of the cruelty which results from an abuse of the opportunities which the present system presents to men, it remains evident that many of the captains of industry who lead men into the field of industrial struggle are using their brains in an effort to better conditions. Their first motives may be even more selfish than those of the military generals, but the results are far more desirable, and humanity secures far better proceeds. They are the leaders in one of the great struggles in the climb toward a more splendid and altruistic civilization and the struggle is fraught with lessons.

Yes, the struggle has its teachings, and that is what we demand. These lessons exemplify the force of human energy, and the value of consistent action. The next great problem for mankind to demonstrate is that of converting the energy of men and the consistency of thoughtful plans into benefits to be derived by the plain toilers themselves as a result of their toil. We concede that the captains at the head of the great industrial trusts were and are the great advance teachers of the world, but humanity has followed long enough. It now ought to be able to direct its own actions, and that must happen before the present problems can be satisfactorily dealt with.

At the present time there is nothing to be gained in war that could not be acquired by some other method. Its results are death, destruction, and despair. In the commercial and industrial field we find elements of production, construction, distribution, and accumulation. The ambitions of the leaders themselves furnish the elements of destruction, but not in the degree in which we find it in the field of war. In the case of war the results of the battle revert to the government of the country that has been successful in the engagement.

The financial kings seek to, and do, secure the substantial profits and the principal products resulting from the labor of the plain toilers. They take their chance in the game of life and gather in the fruits from others' labor. War means destruction and leaves little or nothing to distribute to the soldiers of the ranks, but the activity of men in the field of industry, when applied in connection with the latest mechanical devices, approved methods of application, methods of association, etc., results in an enormous increase in the productive energy of the masses, as well as an enormous daily accumulation of real wealth. But however great the accumulated wealth may be or become, it is a mere bagatelle when compared with the results that must come from the daily expenditure of the energy of the working people, and it is the results of the wealth that is thus brought forth that should be equably distributed, in so far as it can be, to the individuals participating in its production (principally those who labor) as a reward for their industry. They are entitled to it, and in our studies we shall find out why they have not received it. At the same time we shall consider ways and means by which they may, in the future, secure what is properly due to those who honestly, industriously, and intelligently apply themselves.

WHAT IS THE MATTER WITH US?

Business is conducted on a plan that makes it difficult for the most of us to secure the time in which to increase our information and enjoy the appropriate recreations and pleasures that are necessary in order to properly develop our intelligence and give us a correct mental and physical balance. It is true, however, that most of us are, and all men should be, capable of filling better positions in life than most of them occupy, but we are still forced to remain in the same condition because we allow a false system to continue in practice rather than bestir ourselves and enforce the institution of a proper system which would enable us to follow a natural order of things and stop receiving under pay for working over time throughout the entire journey of life.

One reads in newspapers, books, and other sources of information the various views and conclusions of persons very much like ourselves. Some of those who write prove to be capable judges, some poor. Some people judge honestly, some look through clouded glasses and come to strange conclusions. Sometimes the writers are honestly mistaken in their conclusions, but many of them are actually dishonest in the views that they apparently would have other men embrace. One cannot adopt any one of these conclusions as his absolute guide; neither has one the time to read all of them before the necessity arises for him to come to some definite conclusions about present conditions. For that reason I am taking up these studies and inviting all who will to join me. We shall observe at first hand some of the things about which we read. In that way we shall read with our own eyes and by using our own brains be able to understand the daily occurrences that go to make up our lives; understand why there is so much difference in the conditions of people born so nearly alike; judge more truly of actual methods and conditions and reach sane conclusions on which to base our further actions.

A few of us are able to travel a little, some extensively, but the most of us are forced to remain at home. Some men do very little work, but the most of us are forced by present conditions to work all of the time. A few men live by their wits at the expense of mankind as a whole. Some have no wits but are supported by others who have, or by inherited wealth, but the majority of us earn more than we receive and work to support others as well as a system that keeps the most of us overworking and living amid poor conditions. Why is that so? All who will join in making these studies will eventually understand. We shall find evidences of the whole system in every community. We shall recognize them whether our studies extend into distant regions or are confined to our own neighborhood.

If men would candidly consider conditions as they are and as they would be if we were given a square deal, the result would be a united effort to secure a system that would provide the greatest common benefit.

We have three principal thoughts upon which to center our considerations:

First: The actual facts on which the present conditions are based.

Second: The true principles that should have been followed in the formation of our social and industrial systems.

Third: The principles that should now govern in devising and instituting systems that will most successfully promote the general welfare.

The true economic basis is different now from what it would have been if people had, from the beginning, followed a system of social order based on natural conditions. We have been following erroneous practices for generations, and they have finally become a part of our established system. It would not be practical to change immediately to what ought to have been done originally. To do that would bring about such confusion as to defeat the very aims of reform, because there are too many rebels to truth and justice to permit of our going straight to the goal. We would have distress if that were undertaken, such distress that many, perhaps most people, would turn back and defeat reform and become its actual enemies. But there is no reason that can be successfully upheld against our knowing the truth, and after once knowing and understanding it, we should strive to adjust our affairs to what is the true economic basis of our present relations, and seek to reform the present system as rapidly as it can be done without creating social confusion.

I repeat, "social confusion." There is something strange about us as peoples of the earth.

I might say unaccountable. History proves that the people of all nations take pride in their national existence. That is well. It shows that the patriotism of every true lover of his country is the basis on which national existence depends. If a foreign country discriminates against us or offers an insult to our flag or to American citizenship, it brings forth a united response in the form of a demand for justice— simple justice. These demands are sometimes of trifling significance when compared with the injustice and discrimination practised in our own country between our own citizens, the special interests and the plain people, but we back up a demand on a foreign people with the power of our nation. We go to the extent of raising great armies, sacrificing our lives and the treasures of our land, as well as enduring great hardships and confusions of war, in order to sustain what we believe to be our national dignity. That is not strange. Neither is it unaccountable. But lest we confuse the purpose of national existence, the strange and unaccountable thing is that we tolerate the social conditions resulting from the domination of special interests, and become enraged as a nation about external facts that sometimes are of far less importance.

We are stirred by the glitter of brass buttons, uniforms with gold braid, glistening swords, musketry and parade, and all of these are things which might be compared with the toys that are given to children and have no purpose beyond that of the mere satisfaction of a desire for something with which to arouse enthusiasm and amusement. But what about the plain common things, the necessities of daily life, the things that are required in our homes, the necessity for consistent action in our social institutions and the results that come from the expenditure of our energies? We ought to be willing to make great sacrifices in order to secure permanent improvements of the most substantial kind in this respect. But even though we do not, we should at least attempt to put into practice a better system and be willing to endure the temporary confusion that the Money Trust could bring about by forcing a panic in order to retain, if possible, all the most valuable results of our work. As for myself, having studied the relations of these things, I would be willing to endure the confusion, but I recognize from observation that the soldier who will willingly go hungry, risk his life on the battlefield, and leave his family suffering and starving at home, will not endure so much as the temporary flurry that the special interests make every time a substantial reform is undertaken, even though that flurry would give to us the fruits of our energies instead of allowing the interests to continue taking them. But notwithstanding this fact, I am forced to recognize that this attitude of the soldier, and the laborer and people generally, is a condition, and I shall not unduly propose remedies that would bring about even a temporary confusion, although that could be speedily overcome and permanent welfare established by the people if they would positively insist upon the justice in their own rights and interests. I am constrained to go along as slowly as the majority of the people do, but we should not remain ignorant of what ought to be done. Our studies will prove how easily we could accomplish much better results and add to the blessings of life if we were willing to endure for a brief period the financial disturbance of business that the Money Trust can force upon us if we exercise those governmental functions which a dignified people should.

CURRENCY, BANKING, AND THE MONEY TRUST.

There is a man-made god that controls the social and industrial system that governs us. We know him as the "Money Trust." He is offended if given or called by his true name, and being jealous of his power, he opposed an investigation of its sources. At the present time he has an almost illimitable influence upon our daily actions and is seeking to increase it by framing new currency and banking laws to suit his purposes. For that reason our first study will be of the banks and the Money Trust, in order that we may understand their power and the meaning of money.

A few of us have bank accounts, but the most of us have none. Some of us borrow from the banks, but most of us do not and cannot. But, we are all concerned with the accounts and the loans, because they affect business, and, consequently, the conditions of us all. In fact, they control the general business with which we are materially concerned, regardless of our occupation and whether we are rich or poor.

BANKERS PERSONALLY.

Bankers are well-informed and enterprising business men, and are generally good citizens who take a great interest in the welfare of the communities in which they live. They are our acquaintances—the same kind of people that we are, and they generally accommodate and aid us whenever it is possible. That entitles them to a consideration equal to what we expect for ourselves, but they should receive no special favors, and neither should we. They should be under the necessity of responding to the common welfare, and we should be also. But if we were on an equality with them in doing business, we, as well as they, could go on through the journey of life and all would secure better results than even they do now.

It does not require any unusual capacity to become a banker. Any one who possesses ordinary intelligence and common sense can learn to conduct a banking business as easily as he can learn almost any other particular branch of work.

The actual money with which bankers conduct their business belongs largely to the depositors. It is the money that some of us have deposited.

The banks merely loan it out. This money is
used in business and speculation. We shall see
how it is used to control prices. These prices
affect us. We get less for what we sell because
the speculators manipulate the markets against
us, and what we buy costs us more because the
speculators control the prices of commodities.
We take the losses and they take the profits
both ways.

Anyone who can impress the citizens of a
locality with confidence can start a bank. It
has often been done without capital. Even
strangers can present to business men letters of
introduction, and after securing their confidence
and aid, start banks. It is true that permission
must be obtained from the Comptroller of Currency in order to start a national bank, but until
I opened my fight on the Money Trust, even that
had been a mere matter of form, and it is very
seldom that anyone is refused permission when
the application is accompanied by recommendations which are easily obtainable.

BANK CAPITAL.

When a bank is organized the letter of the
law requires that fifty per cent of the capital

should be paid in cash, but that is often a mere matter of form, for the stockholders choose their own directors and officers and sometimes accept their own notes instead of cash. Strings of banks have been organized by individuals associating in that way. Of course, in order to do so, they must in some way secure the confidence of at least a part of the people in the places where they organize, and a sufficient amount of cash with which to pay the expenses of organization and buy the required bonds on which to base bank notes, but temporary loans are often secured for that purpose, and they frequently depend upon the deposits to pay these loans. Further, the law makes it legal to make loans equal to one-tenth of the capital to a single person, and if there are enough associates they are enabled, in addition to borrowing the capital, to borrow the deposits as well, even including the greater part of the reserve, if reserve banks be included in the scheme. Such loans may even be made to certain of the organizers who are without capital.

You might ask, "What are the bank examiners doing if banks can be filled with paper originally worthless? It would require very

many more examiners to be given the time to
learn the value of bank assets; in fact, so many
more that each would have time to tabulate the
assets and make inquiries into the solvency of
the makers of the paper held by the banks.
They would require time to check up and detect
the kiting of notes and accounts going on between those who manipulate that game. Bank
examiners ordinarily visit banks only three or
four times a year, and often examine banks
with even a million dollars assets (consisting of
hundreds, and sometimes thousands, of notes),
list their amounts, subtract payments, count
the cash, and examine the books, all in a day.

Almost all banks, however, organize with substantial capital; that is, what we commonly
accept as such. Banks never start with intent
to defraud depositors. But there is no law to
prevent them from starting without substantial
capital, and they often do. The system itself
has robbed us, and the bankers themselves are
not, as a rule, aware of it. But they are the
beneficiaries of a false system, one that makes
them rich, very rich as a class. Their wealth
is created through a burden placed upon us, and
the wonderment of it all is that we should be so

foolish as to supply other individuals who possess no more intelligence than ourselves, with both the law and the deposits on which to base issues of currency, and systems of credit that tax our life necessities more than all other things combined. That is not an extravagant statement. It is the absolute truth, and the object of our first study is to make it so clear that everyone will understand it.

Banks are not generally organized by the note-kiting system, but they can be, and many are and have been. Even dummy notes are sometimes used, and the extent to which these practices have been resorted to, directly and indirectly, is considerable; but the general public has never realized that it has been done at all.

The law providing for bank capital has been of comparatively little protection to depositors. The bankers themselves have protected their depositors and charged for doing so. Bankers are under the necessity of protecting themselves from failure, and it is due to their diligence and their self-interest that there has been so little direct loss to depositors. Many banks were originally started and capitalized on the paper of individual makers which was worthless at that time, but these banks got our deposits and charged those who borrowed them so much that the profits finally made the paper good. The careful banker usually becomes rich regardless of the fact that he often starts without capital. In other words, the business itself is carried on according to a system which allows the public to be so heavily taxed that failure, generally speaking, is visited on the careless and incompetent only.

It is impossible to determine how many banks started without the actual amount of required capital, but since most banks so started have become financially strong by reason of their accumulated profits, no great good could come from a knowledge of which of the existing solvent banks were originally organized on paper which was actually worthless at the time of the organization. We wish principally to understand the system because it is a false one. Even if the letter and the spirit of the law were followed, still the using of the system is a greater wrong by a thousand times than the mere technical violation of its law. The fact is that our laws are so ridiculous that the bankers have often warped the law to the advantage of the public when it involved no loss to themselves as a consequence.

The Greatest of all our Burdens is the Banking and Currency System.

The speculation and gambling that is incidental to our banking and currency system is simply appalling, and it is absolutely ridiculous that we should tolerate it, and pay the cost of its continuance. Before considering a few of its details let us make a partial review of the burdens that accrue to us as a result. When we examine our losses, even in part only, and see how great is our sacrifice because of our stupendous stupidity in supporting such a system, no doubt we shall be more interested in the manner in which it is operated. Of course it is not a pleasure for one to feel that he has been fooled, but our appetite for information ought to increase when we realize that we could double, yes multiply many times, the advantages we would receive in return for our daily expenditure of energy if a proper system were to be instituted.

It is worth while to know that there are simple remedies which would, if applied, over-

come certain conditions that are immensely
complicated and tremendously cumbersome because of their falsity. It is always easier to
deal in truth and honesty and follow these to
their legitimate ends, than it is to construct
and adjust a false superstructure upon a false
base. But even if no remedy were possible we
should still seek to know about the game that
is being played by the speculating interests.
We certainly do not wish the financially fat
fellows to be able to look beguilingly into our
eyes, and with the concealment of their innermost amusement and delight at our stupidity in
permitting ourselves to be so bamboozled, talk
brazenly about the game that they are playing,
knowing all the time that we do not understand
it. We wish to know the truth about this even
if we do feel humiliated because of our having
previously been ignorant of it.

Here are some figures. In the year ending
June 14th, 1912, the 7,372 national banks cost
us $450,043,250.04 to operate, pay their losses,
dividends, surplus, etc. Up to June 14, 1912,
17,823 State and private banks had reported,
and approximately 4,000 banks had failed to
make any report. The 25,195 reporting banks

operating in 1912 held individual deposits of
$17,024,067,606. Including those not reporting
there were 28,995 banks conducting business in
1912, and the sum it cost the people to operate
these, pay losses, dividends, surplus, etc. (I believe it a conservative estimate) would exceed
$1,300,000,000, or approximately $14 for every
man, woman and child. This is more than it
costs to run the U. S. Government, all things
included. But large as this sum is, it does not
include any report of the operations entered
into by the bankers for their individual consideration. That, no doubt, far exceeds the
mentioned sum, because bankers have unusual
opportunities to speculate and many of them do
speculate on a large scale.

On January 1, 1911, the report of 7,140 national banks showed that they had $1,005,740,-
915 of capital stock paid in, and $662,090,881.82
surplus. The surplus is that part of the profits
not declared as dividends. On September 4th,
1912, there were 7,397 national banks, and their
capital stock was increased to $1,046,012,580,
their surplus to $701,021,452.71, and their un-
divided profits on the last date, less expenses
and taxes, were $242,735,174.37. The dividends

on the stock of national banks in 1912 were
11.66%. But large as these dividends, surplus
and undivided profits are, we have not reached
the climax of this system of extortion.

THE JUGGLING OF CREDITS TO CREATE CAPITAL.

We seem never to have learned the value of
credit or to know that we ourselves form the
basis for it. We are capitalized as so much
stock on hand owned by the trusts. A few of
us get into the deals, some on a small scale, and
a comparatively few on a large scale, and a
half dozen or so have become the real kings of
finance. Of course, it is necessary for the kings
of finance to have scattered throughout the
land underlings who help them gather in the
products of our applied energies, and these in-
voluntary contributions of ours are afterwards
distributed among the favored. Naturally the
underlings are given some crumbs and some of
them even fair slices, but considered in a general way all of the crumbs and slices are distributed in proportion to the capacity the
underlings possess for playing the game well.
The whole loaves are only handled by the kings
of the system, and it is through the expenditure

of our united energy that they are enabled to amass this so-called wealth.

Now, in 1913, there are approximately 30,000 banks. Their number, capital and surplus continually increases. On the basis of that fact the Wall Streeters tell us that the capital of the banks is less concentrated now than it was formerly. They intend by that assertion to lead us to believe that they have less control. I shall prove, however, that the banks are merely the nests from which the Wall Streeters gather the people's financial deposits; that these deposits and the credits built upon their use as a means of amassing capital and levying interest are ever so much more serviceable to the bankers than the capital stock. A large part of the capital stock is consumed in the purchase of fixtures and buildings that serve the banks for offices. The more numerous the banks are, and the more widely scattered through all communities, the greater is the control the Wall Streeters obtain. The people deposit their money in these banks and a large part of the money is used by the Wall Streeters as if they actually owned it, and upon its use they base an enormous credit system.

No bank is organized with the idea that its capital is the basis upon which it secures its main profits. No bank would be organized unless its organizers believed that they could secure the use of the people's savings in a larger amount than the bank's capitalization. Take, for instance, the following six banks in New York City: First National; Chase National; Hanover National; National Bank of Commerce; National City, and National Park. Their deposits on September 4, 1912, amounted to $839,444,142, while their capital stock was only $73,000,000. Approximately the deposits equal 11½ times their capital, exclusive of surplus. Is it not very foxy of them to try to divert our attention from this fact to a consideration of the location of bank capital? When I use the phrase "Wall Streeters" I do not confine it to those having offices in Wall Street. The Wall Street system is maintained in all of the large cities, and I include within the term Wall Streeters all those supporting the Wall Street system, wherever they may be.

In 1900 there were 13,977 banks, which includes non-reporting banks. In 1912 there were 28,995 banks and in that time the deposits increased from $7,688,986,450 to $17,494,067,606. Their surplus increased in a still greater ratio and in the meantime they paid large dividends. It must be apparent to anyone that the money with which to pay the expenses incurred by operating this system (by which I mean to include the whole system of trusts) is collected from the people by capitalizing the products of our energy and even discounting the future in the form of stocks, bonds, and securities issued, on which they collect dividends and interest. This is being accomplished by a reduction of our wages and of the prices for which we sell our products, or the services we render as well as by increasing the price of what they control that we must buy. By inversion this prevents a proper reduction in the hours of labor. These have not decreased, nor has our pay increased proportionately with the new mechanical devices and the new methods of application which have immensely increased our productive energy, but the additional product which has resulted from their use has been capitalized in order that the dividends which we pay shall increase. All of these things were scientifically figured out, then commercialized, then speculatized, and finally gamblerized both as to the present and the future. All have been overdone and all pooled as a common charge against the products accruing from the expenditure of our life's energy.

Many of us were children when the extortion began, and we can hardly blame our parents for permitting the initiation of what we have allowed to be developed into a full-fledged, scientific, legalized system of extortion. But now, since we understand its effects, our children ought to look back on us with shame if we permit its continuance. It is not the bankers who have primarily fastened upon us this system of capitalizing our life energies for their own selfish use. It is the banking and currency system, which we have allowed to remain in operation, and create special interests. The people alone have the power to amend or change it. Therefore we and not the bankers are responsible for the existence of the present system.

Omitting the banks not reporting, of which there were more than 4,000 in 1911, the 25,195 that did report up to June 14, 1912, showed,

Capital stock paid in_____$2,010,843,505.43
Surplus _____ 1,584,981,106.44
Undivided profits _____   581,178,042.47
                              _____
Total accumulations, capital
        included _____$4,177,002,654.34

Over four billion dollars bank capital! That is approximately $44.40 for each man, woman and child, and the bankers actually believe we owe them that, notwithstanding that it is practically a capitalization of ourselves, the same as a farmer capitalizes the growth of his hogs, but with the advantage to the hogs, because the farmer takes good care of the hogs until they are sold to be slaughtered. And what is more, this $44.40 is the nest egg only. We have already paid several times that to them in dividends. But greater than both combined are the profits from the speculation and gambling indulged in by the king bankers, and by many of those to whom they loan the people's deposits. We shall study their operations at another time. The banks are merely the nest eggs of the whole system. Those who gather from these nests have the greatest opportunities.

If we were to look into the banks just before they close, we would find in them persons from the business houses depositing their daily collections. In the earlier banking hours we would find such people making deposits as the farmers, wage earners, and others who do not collect each day the returns of their labor and business affairs.

Out of the 94,000,000 of us, all who are engaged in work or business of any kind for which we receive cash, are trotting immediately to the receiving windows of the 30,000 banks and trust companies and passing over their counters our hard-earned cash. This cash is flowing from these 30,000 banks into Wall Street and other speculating centers like a flood stream. It is the use of these deposits by the speculators that gives the Money Trust its power over the people. Indeed the Wall Streeters have had all the greatest opportunities, for this practice has been going on for a long time.

You may say, "Yes, but the banks loan part of the people's deposits back to them." That is true, but eventually it works out to the satisfaction of the Wall Streeters. Of course, they want enough cash left back in the respective communities from which it pours in, so that our country's industries, whatever they may be, may be operated. That is on the same principle that a farmer will always keep breeders to replenish his live stock. The Wall Streeters know that the harder we work in order to produce commodities of whatever kind, the more we will have to turn over to the rich. The industries must be active everywhere in order to concentrate the cream of their products into the vaults of the banks and finally into the control of the trusts and special interests. In our studies this will become as plain as the noonday sun on a clear day.

Yes, there are 30,000 banks in the small towns, villages, and great cities, that serve as nests into which the eggs are dropped,—that is, our cash. The total of our individual deposits for the year of 1912, in the banks making reports to the Comptroller of Currency, was $17,024,-067,606. Add to that the deposits in banks not reporting, and the total will be correspondingly increased. That enormous amount was supplied by us as a result of the expenditure of our energy and labor, and it is important that we should know what good, if any, comes from our supplying these banks with working material to be used under the present system.

Banks are divided into three classes:

First, New York, Chicago, and St. Louis form a class by themselves, and are called the Central Reserve Banks.

Second, 47 of the other large cities are Reserve Cities, and in those, banks are designated as Reserve Banks.

Third, all of the banks not in the first two classes are called Non-Reserve Banks.

This classification gives the greatest elasticity to the system of speculating and gambling with the deposits. It is this classification also that gave the Money Trust its start. It secured the use of the people's money just the same as if it had actually owned it. How, you ask? . . . . Simple enough! It is worked by a rule of self interest—profit to the banks. The law requires the non-reserve banks to keep 15% reserve. This they are prohibited from loaning to borrowers in the locality from which the banks get their deposits, but they may keep 3/5 (or over half) of it in reserve banks, and the latter may loan 75% of that 3/5 out to anybody. Further, the Reserve Banks offer the Non-Reserve Banks 2% interest and that inducement secures for them the greater part of these reserves, and much of the time even more than is required for the reserve.

The Reserve Banks are required to keep 25% reserve, but all except those in the three Central Reserve Cities, New York, Chicago and St. Louis, may keep 50% of their reserves in these three cities. From this it will be seen that a practical working out shows that the actual reserves of the banks are, in non-reserve banks, approximately 6% of their deposits; and in the other banks, except New York, Chicago and St. Louis, 12½% of their deposits. The rest is principally sent to the banks in Central Reserve cities which pay 2% interest and loan it out largely to speculators and promoters.

To those not knowing the tricks of the business, the practice of keeping reserves in other banks may seem harmless. But upon examination we find it to be a most clever device, and operated in order that the banks generally shall supply the financial speculators and gamblers with the people's money. It is true that that is not the real purpose of most bankers, but it results in that.

Editorials in that portion of the press that is subservient to the Money Trust, state that we plain people have billions of dollars deposited in the banks, and seek to make the list of depositors appear to be a general one. But any one person having deposits in two or more banks was listed as many times as his name appeared in the list of depositors in different banks, and some business houses have hundreds of accounts in one form or another. After this process they boldly proceed to ask, "Who is the Money Trust?" . . . This is their brazen answer to their own question: "The people are." Thousands of newspapers are supported by the interests for the very purpose of beguiling us into believing the things that these interests want us to believe. This question of who owns and who uses the money is the one on which they expend the greatest efforts in order to deceive.

It is a fact that the people own a part of the bank deposits, but the banking system is so cleverly arranged in the interest of the banks that the people have comparatively little benefit from their own deposits. On the contrary, the people's money placed in the banks is principally used as a basis for credit and on that credit the banks collect the interest which operates to reduce the prices of what we sell and increase the prices of what we buy.

General business is transacted on approximately $24 credit to each dollar in cash, . . . and under the highly specialized system of Wall Street there is a still greater elasticity of credit. ¡We all know that business is not carried on wholly with the actual money, in fact, business is almost wholly conducted on credit.

Yes, . . . the people do own considerable of the money deposited in the banks, but they do not use the credit that is based upon it. They deposit the money, but the banks in conjunction with the speculators, appropriate and manipulate the credit based upon that. We support that credit and during normal times that practice has a vastly greater effect in the ` control of business than does the actual money. That is where we plain folks get left. If any of us wish to use the credit we must pay the banks 6% and upwards, and yet the value of that same credit is based upon the products of our own energy. The banks do not, ordinarily, part with the money when they make loans. The borrower gives his note and the sum for which it calls is placed to his credit on the bank books, after which he checks on that account to pay bills. These checks are usually deposited by the payee in the same or some other bank and in the general average of business each bank gets back as much as it loans. The money that we deposit forms the basis for an amount of credit many times greater than the amount of actual money. The bankers have the advantage of all that, . . . and it is pyramided and sold and resold many times. The banks are specialists in the manipulation of that credit and as a matter of fact they are required by the exigencies of business to be so, as long as we allow the present ridiculous system of money and credit supply to continue.

On June 14, 1912, all told, there was only $1,572,953,579.43 of actual money in the reporting banks, but in these same banks there was credited to individual depositors over seventeen billions. The banks have never had, at one time, much in excess of one and one-half billion dollars of real money.

The banks are properly the clearing houses for money and credit exchanges, but they have misapplied their trust and have become our commercial masters. Many of them have associated

themselves with the gambling speculators and
are now speculating for themselves. Further,
the people's deposits are being used by them
and those to whom they loan to pyramid in
stocks, bonds, and other securities, which aggregate at the present time approximately amounts
to $50,000,000,000 and is rapidly nearing the
$100,000,000,000 mark. Excessive dividends and
interest are charged and compounded semi-
annually and annually on this sum. That de-
creases our net earnings, increases the price of
the commodities we buy, and prevents a proper
reduction in the hours of labor required.
Against this $50,000,000,000 on which the Money
Trust combination charges us exorbitant maintenance expense, in addition to interest and
dividends, we own merely a part of the $17,000,-
000,000 of deposits, and a few of us are drawing
3% and 4% interest on small balances.

You can now begin to appreciate how comparatively insignificant the little deposits a few of
us plain folks are able to make for ourselves
are, when we measure the interest we get with
the maintenance expense, dividends, interest
and profits which the bankers, trusts, and speculators obtain on the credits they create on these

deposits, and realize that all of these are supported by the products of our energy expenditure.

To give a concrete illustration, take, for instance, the increasing reserves held by the following central reserve banks: Hanover National, National City, National Bank of Commerce, First National Bank, and Chase National. These are the six principal banks in New York City and we can apply the principle that governs them with that which governs other banks without going into tiresome details. Covering a period of 15 years, notice how diligently they have been skimming the country for the reserves of other banks. The growth of these reserves held by the six banks are as follows for the period named:

September, 1898	$ 94,394,210
September, 1899	154,514,691
September, 1900	176,731,918
September, 1901	216,763,488
September, 1902	253,515,055
September, 1903	227,780,147
September, 1904	258,558,149
August, 1905	291,732,471
September, 1906	334,560,214
August, 1907	336,553,788
September, 1908	311,499,877
September, 1909	399,658,140

September, 1910...................... 400,740,817
September, 1911...................... 451,050,573

The capital of these six banks has been increased from time to time during the last fifteen years by means of adding a part of their profits. In 1912 it was $73,000,000 (the larger part of which was the profits that had been previously made on a smaller capitalization), and in addition they had $82,000,000 surplus; in other words, profits piled up. Besides all that, they had $26,332,698 of undivided profits, or profits that have not been declared as dividends or placed to the credit of surplus. In the meantime, these six banks had paid enormous dividends to the stockholders. The profits of the First National, one of the banks mentioned above, amounted to $86,000,000 in fifty years. The original investment was $500,000. The total deposits of the "Big Six" now, in 1913, approximates a billion dollars. We should not overlook the fact that this is largely actual money, as the New York banks secure more of that than banks elsewhere, and that by Wall Street's system of credits it may support many billions of credits for the Wall Streeters.

There is a group of banks in each of the large

cities working the same game with the credit supported by the people, and yet, enormous as the aggregate amount of these bank profits may seem, they are almost insignificant when compared with profits that we pay the other special interests which have grown out of our monstrous banking and currency system.

We now have fixed, as a part of our knowledge, the fact that bankers have by law and by practice special privileges which enable them to handle the people's money and juggle with credits in such a way that they become rich, but we have not yet seen the greatest of their advantages. We have already found that bankers as a class are rich, made rich by the use of the credit that is supported by us, and they are organized for the very purpose of using that.

We should mention something about the personalities of the bankers whom we meet upon the journey of life, and strive to learn by what rule or right, they secure the privilege of converting into their own control the credit that is necessary in order to carry on the business and commerce of the country. Why should the bankers have the power to contract and expand at their pleasure, the credit that the people themselves

support? Under the present order of civilization it is the greatest privilege in existence.
The manner of its exercise by bankers and speculators is continually sending to their graves
thousands of poverty-stricken persons for each
person that it aids to competency. Is it not
extremely important that we should know by
what method these bankers become the arbiters
of our destinies? They were not selected by us
to do this. Just so long as we allow them to
dominate by the system they employ, the road
to success is absolutely closed to the vast
majority of farmers, wage earners, and others
employed in different pursuits of life.

In the earlier part of our study we made some
observations about bank capital. We are now
prepared to know more about it. In order to
obtain the controlling advantage in the banking
business, it is not sufficient to own a little bank
stock. Many people own bank stock and some
control banks without knowing much about their
actual power. These, however, are the ordinary
banks, such as most of us patronize if we have
occasion to do a direct business with banks.
These banks serve as supply stations for the
larger city banks. They are not designed for

that purpose, but that is the result of the system under which they operate.

We have already observed that any person of ordinary capacity, bearing a fair reputation, and possessing actual nerve, can start a bank, without capital, in any place where a bank is needed, and that they frequently do at points where no additional bank is necessary. We have also learned that the greater part of the banking capital has been created out of profits obtained from the use of the people's labor and credit; that the surplus of the six largest New York banks exceeds their stated capital, it being $73,000,000, while the surplus is $82,000,000; that much of their stated capital was created out of earlier surplus accounts; and that, in addition, they have $26,332,698 of undivided profits. What is commonly thought of as actual capital is simply the notes, or the proceeds from the notes, of some of the principal incorporators who borrowed from banks, or from others, and paid them with money out of the dividend collections. The whole thing is, and has been, based almost entirely upon a system of credit, and we have remained ignorant of the fact that instead of allowing a few men with average capacity, supposed fair reputation, and actual nerve, to appropriate the credit that the rest of us have supported by hard labor, we should have utilized that credit for the benefit of those plain people who really support it.

We should become firmly imbued with the truth of that statement. Indeed, the most of us who are over 21 years old and have voted will become more and more humiliated as we proceed and realize how we have been beguiled into supporting the very things that have robbed us of the best results of our life's energy. But it is better to be once humiliated and become thereafter ashamed of our own past stupidity, than it is to continue in ignorance and place the increasing burdens upon the shoulders of our children. It is time that we realized that our banking and currency system is not only rotten in its application but that it is absolutely false in its basis, and must be changed.

It is because of that condition that I introduced a resolution providing for an investigation of the Money Trust. The interests saw the danger in which such an investigation would place them if the public should learn the actual facts, and they immediately started that portion

of the press controlled by the trusts to laughing
at my resolution. An attempt was made by
those interests and the subservient political
bosses, irrespective of party, to ridicule it out
of Congress. They recognized that the resolution was aimed at the very heart of all the
trusts and combinations.

The political bosses do not always keep so
well informed about the ways of business as
they do about the jugglery of politics, nor the
means by which the public may be prevented
from understanding their operations, but they
do juggle the rules of both Houses of Congress
in order to restrain action against and promote
action favorable to the trusts. The trusts in-
form the politicians of how they wish them to
act upon matters which affect the trusts, and in
the case of my resolution they were induced to
pigeon-hole it. But the public had heard the
alarm. The independent press was insistent on
information . . . sought to obtain facts
from me, searched for other facts themselves
. . . and heralded to the world the purposes
of the resolution. Thousands of letters and
telegrams were sent to the Members of Congress from their constituents. . . . The polit-

ical bosses soon found it necessary to cover the tracks the trusts had made when coming to their offices. . . . Something had to be done, and that quickly, or the indignation aroused at the failure of Congress to act would run riot and the heads of political bosses tumble.

Secret meetings were held by the representatives in Congress of the trusts and bosses. The doors of the innermost and least suspected offices were barred to the public, and so guarded that none should enter who were interested on behalf of the public. In these offices plans were laid for the drafting of a new resolution, the purpose of which was to defeat the appointment of a special committee, and to substitute for it the Banking and Currency Committee, which was chiefly composed of bankers, their agents and attorneys, and the interests expected that that committee would faithfully protect the wrongs committed against the public, in so far as it could be done without arousing public suspicion. It could not whitewash the whole of the Money Trust operations, but much could and would be concealed by that means, and was in fact, as was shown by subsequent developments.

The next step was to secure the passage

of this substituted resolution, which really
amounted to the investigation being made by
the secret friends of the Money Trust. This
committee, as well might be expected, . . .
because of the special personal interest of its
members, . . . did not select an attorney to
aid them from among the many able attorneys
who are Members of the House and who would
serve without further pay than that to which
they are entitled as Members, ... but they
selected a Wall Street attorney, paid him a very
high salary, allowed him to manage the whole
investigation and practically draft the committee's report. I do not make that statement as a
reflection upon the attorney so selected, but
merely to indicate the fact that the Banking
and Currency Committee did not view this subject from the standpoint of the general public.

At first it was supposed that the public would
be appeased with such a proceeding, and the
whole subject be easily handled under the sacred
boss system. A secret caucus was resorted to.
. . . In a later study we shall consider these
secret caucuses and ascertain the method by
means of which the politicians have so long

served the trusts while being maintained in office by the public.

The caucus on the Money Trust resolution was attended by many well-meaning but misguided followers of bossism. The substituted Money Trust Resolution was adopted, and on a later day passed by the House. Those Members who bound themselves by the gag caucus rule were guilty of perjury and treason, but that has been so common a result of the caucus rule that it is no longer considered as such by them. They believe that anything founded in precedent is justified, and each believes that he is justified and his conscience satisfied when once he yields his convictions to the will of the bosses. But the people will awaken their asphyxiated consciences on this caucus system once they learn the cost it entails on national efficiency.

The Money Trust won, . . . of course, . . . and the Banking and Currency Committee took charge of the investigation on behalf of their masters, the bankers. Probably not one of the men on this committee is really dishonest. I believe that each one of them believes that he is conscientious and that he does not intentionally wrong the public. But they have developed the selfish viewpoint to a degree that enables them to believe that the public is really mistaken. That is almost always the case, however, with those who have become the beneficiaries of a system.

The Banking and Currency Committee had to be forced by public opinion to do more than make a pretense at action. It was presumed by its members that the public was ignorant of the facts, but the truth was that too many things had already been exposed. The public demanded proof. A great political party was in danger. The bosses saw the danger and they made a feint at investigation, as a result of which they gathered in a few morsels to be spread broadcast before the general election. Then all was silent and the committee would meet and adjourn, and meet again and adjourn, and so on, over and over again. While that continued the Money Trust and the subservient politicians were safe. All was quiet until Congress convened. Then, on December 2, 1912, I introduced the following resolution:

WHEREAS, Congress created in 1908 a National Monetary Commission with authority to investigate monetary problems in general, and

WHEREAS, said Committee has been discharged, but first made and filed a report and recommendations for certain legislation embodied in a bill now pending in Congress and popularly known as the Aldrich plan, but the report failed to disclose any facts in relation to the monopolistic control exercised by certain great special interests of the principal money and credit that enters into commerce, business, and speculation; and

WHEREAS, it is vital that Congress should know the facts relating thereto before permanent remedial financial legislation should be undertaken, and

WHEREAS, there is a pressing demand for early legislation, and for other good and sufficient causes, the House authorized the Banking and Currency Committee to investigate the Money Trust, which exercises a potential and injurious influence in the control of the principal sources of money and credit supply entering commerce, business and speculation, and

WHEREAS, the Committee, in the many months that have passed since it was so authorized, seems not to have undertaken the investigation for the purpose of securing facts to aid in framing early remedial financial legislation, but rather to have been planning an investigation as if for indictment or some other remote purpose, and in which it is blocked by offenders against honest and impartial rules of business and Government officials who deem the personal privileges of banks so sacred that their business shall not be inquired into even for the benefit of the public, and

WHEREAS, this action on the part of the special interests, supported by the refusal of the Government officials to help the committee, is important in itself, the facts should become a part of the committee report, but should in no way delay the investigation which is important in that its purpose is to secure the facts and circumstances that improperly interfere with legitimate commerce and business. If the committee intends to secure information for other purposes and has not sufficient power, it nevertheless should secure the information which is of the most vital importance and which was the moving cause for its authorization; that is, information which will enable Congress to intelligently enact remedial laws relating to the control of money and credits; and

WHEREAS, it has never been claimed that there is or ever was an organized or even an unorganized association that can be specifically pointed to and named as the Money Trust, it is therefore useless to undertake to prove such an organization exists for the purpose of punishing it. Neither formal nor informal organization is necessary to its potential existence. In fact, its power is the greater because it exists without actual material rules of organization, for by the methods of its existence it is immune from prosecution. It nevertheless can and does by indirection what it could not do by direction. The very fact that the business interests know that there is a money power which can make or unmake business for them gives that power its greatest efficiency of control. Silently and surely that power is exerted, and its force is realized by all industrial agencies. Because of its peculiar, yet potent, force, it is important that we have early legislation. The main facts and circumstances by which the Money Trust is maintained may be easily proven to the intelligence and understanding of the public by a proper compilation of the facts that are now obtainable, and it was for that purpose principally

that the committee received its authority from
the House; Now, therefore, be it
RESOLVED, That the Committee on Banking and
Currency is requested to proceed without delay
with an investigation of the Money Trust influence, for the purpose of securing all the practical information and data that may reasonably
be had in regard to the influence exercised by
the Money Trust in the control of banks and
of money and credits.
RESOLVED FURTHER, That said committee
shall report the results of its investigation to
the House from time to time with reasonable
promptness.

The press immediately published broadcast
the substance of the above resolution. As a
result of the strong public sentiment, the committee was forced to act with more diligence.
(The same as the politicians in the old political
parties became progressive when public opinion
forced it.) The party in control scented danger.
The fear of adverse public sentiment, the only
thing that boss politicians fear, aroused them to
action. The committee was now forced to sub-
pœna witnesses and hear their testimony, some
parts of which were afterwards published by
the press.

In the speech that I made in support of my
first resolution, I disclosed the conditions that
the subsequent evidence of the kings of finance

proved to exist. . . . But the committee soft-
pedaled, and brought out only those things that
every student of the financial conditions already
knows, and such information as had been substantially published in magazines and discussed
in Congress by Senator LaFollette, myself, and
others. It was only the fact that it was furnished verbally by the fellows in the actual
game that aroused a new and more general
interest.

The committee did not seek out the most
crafty arts of these speculators and gamblers in
order that the public might secure a correct
view of the false system of laws that govern
the banking and currency business; but what
was to be expected from a committee that was
controlled by bankers, and whose chairman was
a banker? . . . Naturally, it avoided questions upon the most important economic truths
which should have been disclosed as a result of
the investigation. The tricks of the witnesses
will die with them, but the system that permits
the tricks still remains for others to operate
under until it shall be remedied.

A sub-committee was created to propose a
remedy. This committee is also controlled by

the bankers, and has a banker for chairman.
These men have personal financial interests in
the legislation. Our—that is, the peoples'—
concern in changing the system is to promote the
general welfare. . . . The bankers have a
special interest, and since they control the committee, . . . what show have we against
them? Since their interest is to collect interest
from us! . . . They go as far as they dare
without arousing a hurricane of public indignation as a result of the favors they extend to their
own business. [The friendliness that the Banking and Currency Committee displayed toward
the Money Trust was apparent to anyone who
had given any time to the study of the problems
placed before it for investigation. Their work
was as mere play when compared with the importance of the subject.] Nevertheless, it served
a good purpose, although its service was of a
weak nature.

[Jacob H. Schiff, one of New York's greatest
financiers, and one of the witnesses who testified
before the committee, is an example of a man
with the kind of mind and overselfish viewpoint
which prevails among the men who had a personal financial interest in the result of the Com-

mittee's investigation, such as the banker members of the Banking and Currency Committee may be expected to have. Mr. Schiff, under oath, told the committee in substance that:

"If individuals can accomplish a monopoly he believed they should not be hampered by law! The laws of nature, he told the committee, are best for preventing too gigantic projects; and he cited the fall of the Tower of Babel as an example of the futility of human effort extended too far. Among the articles expounded by Schiff in his creed of business and finance was the assertion that the minority in all corporations should not be allowed representation among the officers and directors by law. 'The majority should always rule,' he said, 'and the minority should protect their rights as best they can.'"

Is it not easy to see by this statement of Mr. Schiff's that it is preposterous for Congress to appoint mostly bankers, their agents and attorneys on its Banking and Currency Committee? Mr. Schiff is not cut from a different cloth, nor by a different pattern than the rest of humanity. Acting in our individual capacity, we look after our own interests, but in a collective sense we have not carried this interest far enough, and, consequently, we have such financial wizards as Mr. Schiff.

Now, let us analyze the last sentence of the quotation from Banker Schiff's testimony to his brother bankers when the committee examined him. He said:

"The majority should always rule and the minority should protect their rights as best they can."

Now suppose we consider our own case—that is, the interests of the public—in the light of this statement of a king banker, which statement bears reference to the smaller stockholders in corporations. There are 30,000 banks in this country. There may be 200,000 bankers. I do not know their exact number, but I know that there are approximately 94,000,000 of us. In the percentage of human beings the bankers are not equal to 1 per cent of the population. There is, on the average, perhaps not more than one banker to 2,000 other people. Suppose we should take Mr. Schiff at his word and let the minority "protect their interests as best they can," and we, the people, take the power which we possess,—and the Constitution contemplates that we should exercise as a government, and Lincoln proposed, . . . namely, "coin the people's national credit," . . . instead of letting the bankers coin it for their own selfish use. What would happen to Mr. Schiff and his

brother bankers who control the Committee on
Banking and Currency if we did that? . . .
That is one of the questions that will be an-
swered before this study ends.

THE ALDRICH PLAN.

Lest the purpose of my starting the original
Money Trust probe be misconstrued, I here
state that it was not for the purpose of dis-
covering the Money Trust. Long before that
time it was known by those who had carefully
studied the problem that there was a money
power combination that operated and controlled
the country's finances and carried on its operations in a shameful manner. The purpose and
actual effect of my original resolution was a
flank move, to defeat the special interests in
their attempt to fasten on the people of this
country the so-called Aldrich Banking and Currency Plan for 50 years. This plan was an
attempt on their part to make the greatest steal
from the people that has ever been made.

In the panic of 1903 I began taking notice
of the operations of the larger banks. At that
time, as far as I could see, there had been no
attempt to form combinations in order to cen-

tralize deposits. Each banker seemed to be working out his separate business existence along that line, and at the same time getting all that he could in return. There were, however, banking associations which brought the bankers together, and in these meetings they discussed ways and means for their mutual advantage—even to the extent of maintaining efficient influence over legislation.

Ever since the Civil War, Congress has allowed the bankers to completely control financial legislation. The membership of the Finance Committee in the Senate and the Committee on Banking and Currency in the House, has been made up of bankers, their agents and attorneys. These committees have controlled the nature of bills to be reported, the extent of them, and the debates that were to be held on them when they were being considered in the Senate and the House. No one, not on the Committee, is recognized under the practice of the House as long as a member on the committee wishes recognition, and one of them is sure to hold the floor unless someone favorable to the committee has been arranged for. In this way the committees have been able to do as they pleased.

The men who have appointed the committees in the last 50 years have not had the clear and earnest viewpoint of our forefathers. On Tuesday, January 14, 1794, the following resolution was introduced in the U. S. Senate:

Quotation "A."—"Nor shall any person holding any office or stock in any institution in the nature of a bank, for issuing or discounting bills or notes payable to bearer or order, under the authority of the United States, be a member of either House whilst he holds such office or stock."

It passed the Senate two days later, after being fought by the bankers, and amended at their instigation in order that they might be allowed to sit in Congress, but it still remained a protest to bankers controlling legislation in which they were personally interested. At the present time we possess a dulled and worn appreciation of the general fitness and consistency of these things, and we have surrendered all of our finances, including the actual control of legislation in Congress to the bankers, their agents and attorneys. At the earlier date above stated, when people were less commercial and more ethical than now, . . . they feared to trust

the bankers even as plain Members of Congress.
We of this age allow them to absolutely control
all of the committees in Congress that make
the laws of finance. Some of the members of
these committees belong to banking associations
that lobby in Congress in order to secure action
favorable to the bankers. Are we satisfied that
the bankers to whom we pay enormous tributes
from our very life's necessities, . . . should
control finar.:ial legislation? . . . Shall the
Senate and House continue to give the representatives in Congress who are supported by
the financial usurers a monopoly of the committees that deal with this most important subject? . . . Shall the people supinely pay the
constantly increasing usury, and still cheer their
popularly elected representatives for permitting
bankers to control the bills that are to be reported to the House, as well as the debates on
them? . . . Are the people to have no hearing
on the questions of banking, currency, and
usury?

On two different occasions within the last two
years I have, by the introduction of resolutions,
called the attention of Congress to the fact that
no Senator or Representative should be a mem-

ber of a committee that controls or influences legislation in which he has a personal interest, and especially that no banker should be on either of the committees controlling financial legislation.   But Congress, notwithstanding such notice, has failed to act, and goes right on filling up the committees with members who are personally financially interested in the legislation that their committees control, and even appointing such members chairmen of the committees.

In 1893 the large Wall Street banks, and the large affiliating banks in other centers, determined to make some changes in the banking and currency laws, and especially in regard to the purchase of silver by the Government.   They began by creating a stringency which we shall refer to later.   It resulted in a general business and financial scare to all of the smaller banks and the business interests.   It became a real panic which continued with its disastrous results for a period of years.   During that period the special interests squeezed many of the small banks and some large ones, and some of these, and many business concerns, were forced into bankruptcy.   Time and time again before that the bankers had been able to secure many special favors from Congress. But even with all these to their advantage they had some sleepless nights during that panic. They went through an experience that gave them further suggestions as to what would be required in their interests in the way of legislation. Immediately they began to form powerful affiliations among themselves in order to further protect themselves against the disadvantages of panics. But instead of seeking safety for themselves and protection for the general public by means of a modification of the methods of the banking business, as a reward for the special favors that had been given to them by Congress, they did not consider for a moment the protection of the public, but sought diligently for a method by which they could secure the privilege of fleecing the public whenever a panic should be in progress. That is, they would have panics, if they did occur, profitable to the favored bankers and disastrous to the public, and a panic may happen at any time under present conditions. As a matter of fact the bankers may cause a panic whenever the public seeks to enforce its rights.

In the last twenty years the banking business has grown enormously. About 1898 the signs of affiliation between the larger and more powerful banks and trust companies began to multiply. It is doubtful if at that time there was any intention on the part of the active management of the banks to associate together for any but legitimate purposes. Their affiliation was due principally to the fact that the wily heads of the big business and speculative interests decided to buy in bank stocks with a view to controlling their deposits in order that they might possess the means with which to exploit the people. They were after the deposits, and the ownership of the bank stock was necessary if they were to accomplish their purpose, but, it was merely incidental.

About the year 1900 there was some open talk of combinations being favored between the larger banks in New York City and some of the large trust companies in that and other cities. Steps were also taken to link with those interests the largest of the life insurance companies. That is why J. P. Morgan & Co. bought the control of a great life insurance company. Cash was coming in to the companies from the policyholders everywhere. The interests, of course, wished to control that. Combinations of various kinds rapidly increased to include all of the greater concerns in large cities as well as many of the concerns in smaller towns, and in many cases it included even those in the villages. The large operators do not enter extensively into the ownership of the small institutions. These are controlled through a mutuality of business interests. Employees are frequently given the control of the smaller concerns. One can easily understand why this same selfish purpose of making the biggest profits possible causes institutions, separately owned, to co-operate as completely as they do when the stock ownership is identically the same.

The consequence is that the capitalists and financiers of Wall Street who do their "High Finance" stunts and are known as "Big Business" now dominate the banking system. It requires a little patience for those not familiar with business methods generally, to understand the facts and their bearings as they are presented, but since we know that a knowledge of these things will make us more successful in a business way, make our lives better, happier, and more intelligent, and require of us less hours of labor, and give us more equable returns for our labor, we should not fail to give a great deal of attention to the subject. If once convinced that it intimately concerns our daily existence, we will do so.

We shall not take the time to review the scandals that grow out of the Wall Street control of the funds of the life insurance companies and the manipulation of the finances by insiders. All this manipulation is done in order to compel the liquidation of many solvent banks, and industrial as well as transportation companies. We already know that it has caused numerous suicides and other desperate acts on the part of the owners and managers. These things serve as examples of what occurs to those who dare to disobey the command of the financial kings. Many of the men at the head of, or managing big business interests, possess the spirit of friendliness toward all the people of the world, but they, too, in many cases have been forced to fall into line.

Neither verbal or written contract is necessary for the existence of a money trust. The power to punish without trial is a sufficient weapon in the hands of the money kings. The late J. Pierpont Morgan swore that he did not loan money on security, however perfect or valuable it might be, unless he knew the borrowers personally or had an individual knowledge that satisfied him. That was the substance of his statement before the Money Trust Committee in December, 1912. Mr. Morgan was the world's greatest banker. Many of the institutions that he controlled have had special privileges conferred upon them by the Government and yet this king of bankers, who was financially the most powerful in the world, proved by his testimony given under oath, that the institutions controlled by him and to which the public, through its Congressmen (who are subservient to his and other special interests), have surrendered a sacred trust,—this man, by his statement proved that he was only partially performing the trust when he stated that he refused money to all who were not known to him— known, you will understand, by the law of selfish interest to be subservient to J. P. Morgan & Co. It mattered not how honest the applicants, or how much or how valuable their security. They had to be known to be sub-

servient to that firm. If that is not a proof of
partiality in the application and business administration of the law, and the trust reposed
in banks, when we give them special privileges,
—then, by the great heavens, what proof do we
want? It shows that they have the power, and
Banker Morgan did choose to exercise it. The
others who were associated with him had to do
the same thing as he, or he did not accept them
as associates. Others who were associated with
J. P. Morgan & Co. naturally followed the same
practice. By that method it passed along, and
with a comparatively few exceptions there is
favoritism from the dominant to the servient,
and the rest of us are only goats.

How easy it is to understand the Money Trust
when we catch the spirit of Morgan's answer,
and when we realize its resources we begin to
understand the silent but no less effective force,
which commands, without word or act to which
we can point specifically and say, "This is the
identified power." The refusal of a loan to
those who would secure it because they were not
favorably known to bow to the king banker was
sufficient proof. Shall we, notwithstanding that
fact, continue to allow the banks to control the

finances, a power which the Constitution gives to the government only? Banks may properly conduct the financial transactions between the people and receive a reasonable compensation for the service, but should neither control the legislation nor the issue of money.

Of course, no one who has given the subject proper study claims that there is an organized or even an unorganized association that can be specifically pointed to and named as the Money Trust, but formal organization is not necessary to its potential existence. As a matter of fact, its power is greater because it exists without organization. It gains its purposes by indirection more effectively than it could by direction. It derives its greatest efficiency from the very fact that the business interests are aware of the existence of a power which can make or unmake them at its will. Silently and grimly, that power is exerted, and it is recognized and felt by all of the industrial interests of today.

That is a condition, and while I do not spare my criticism of the system, I do not blame such men as Mr. Morgan was, nor do I blame any of the bankers, because they are doing the things that are quite natural for human beings to do when opportunity is presented without limitations. For the sake of argument let us try to see as Mr. Morgan did and consider these facts from the viewpoint that he probably took. None of us will have the opportunity to do what he did in his time, because when we really understand we will not permit anyone to fleece us as J. P. Morgan & Co. and other bankers have fleeced us.

Surely when we see how these bankers have impoverished us by selling to us,—at usury prices,—the credit that is supported by our own toil, we will demand the privilege of controlling that credit for ourselves. We are willing to pay the bankers for their actual services, and for the skill which they exercise in facilitating exchange that is incidental to the legitimate commerce of the country, but further than that we are not obligated.

The king bankers put in motion, in 1907, a great scheme. They had gambled and speculated on Wall Street until so many watered stocks and bonds had been manufactured on speculation, that numberless speculators, big and small, sprang up all over the country, and stocks, bonds, and credits were pyramided, and re-pyramided, and re-re-pyramided. Of course such a condition could not last and a crash was inevitable, because it was not natural for such gambling to continue.

The largest crop ever grown, up to that time, was harvested in 1907 and all of the natural conditions were favorable to the greatest prosperity,—but speculation, unnatural and false, had expanded to a point where it offset all of the natural advantages. The king bankers knew the conditions and informed the most favored of their friends what was to come.

There was to be a panic in the fall of 1907 that would be advertised as the result of our bad banking and currency laws. They are bad, we admit, but it was the general speculation and the manipulations of the king bankers that was directly responsible for the panic. The bad laws were merely used as an excuse for covering their acts. But while that is the truth, it does not settle the question. We must make laws to fit the people, for we cannot make people to fit the laws. Ever since civilization began, that has been tried without success. The so-called "trust busters," who generally have been former attorneys for the trusts, do make a pretense of trying it, but they often secure their government retainers through politicians subservient to the trusts, and educated as they are in the interests of the trusts, we cannot expect much from their efforts. None of their prosecutions have resulted in lessening the cost of living. It is rather strange that anyone would believe that the cost of living will be lessened by the prosecution of the trusts. Prosecutions will serve only to establish the majesty of the law. They will not remedy the high cost of living.

We have already stated that an enormous amount of watered stock, bonds and securities were issued prior to 1907. The old laws had aided the trusts in the manufacture of these, but at that time they decided that they must have new laws favorable to their operations if they were to aggrandize and monetize their securities as they wished. They had indeed secured great holdings—the largest ever. This 1907 panic was to be the means by which the people were to be forced to enact new laws, guaranteeing the full face value of the watered stocks and bonds. That guarantee would make the people pay the interest and dividends on them forever. By this method the greatest steal ever contemplated since the beginning of humanity would be accomplished. Thus, in 1907, when Nature had responded most bountifully and when there was due to us the greatest prosperity, we were given a panic as the initial move for the proposed steal,—the Aldrich Plan.

That portion of the press subsidized by the Money Trust blamed the panic to the bad banking and currency laws. A majority of the independent press unwittingly fell into the trap and helped the interests by also blaming the laws. The failure of the latter to express the truth about it is accountable to the fact that it requires more study to understand the banking and currency laws than most editors have the time or opportunity to give on short notice. All, except the few who had been prepared for the panic, suffered more or less loss and struck back at random without really knowing what or who to blame or hit at. That is what the special interests wanted them to do. It is not strange, is it, that most people criticized the laws to which the beguiling trusts,—the Money Trust particularly—cunningly pointed as the cause?

It did not seem to occur to many that these were the same laws under which the trusts

have been enabled to acquire their fortunes and
to which they had given their former praise.
But now the fortunes of these interests had
become so very large that the great advantages
given them under the laws no longer satisfied
their increasing greed, and for that reason they
sought to modify the laws and greatly increase
their advantages.

Accordingly, when Congress convened bills
were introduced to amend the banking and currency laws. The 1907 panic had been a force-
ful reminder to the people that a change was
needed, but what kind of a change it should be,
they had not the opportunity to investigate for
themselves in the short time given them in
which to decide upon the nature of the bill to
be adopted. That fact was relied upon by the
Money Trust, and the bill that finally passed
was kept from the public notice until it became
a law. It was purposely kept back, the intention being to spring it at the opportune time
and rush it through.

Nelson W. Aldrich, whom the politicians of
Rhode Island had sent to Congress as their
Senator, took charge in the Senate, and Edward
B. Vreeland, a prominent banker who was elect-

ed by the voters of the 37th Congressional District of New York to Congress, took charge in the House. These two distinguished gentlemen protected well the cause of the banks.

In every session of Congress much time is deliberately wasted on nothingness and frivolity. Members make partisan political speeches and do all sorts of monkey work,—over half of the time is absolutely wasted. Sometimes a single Member will take an hour on a so-called "question of personal privilege." But when great problems involving our fundamental rights are up before the House for consideration, the time for debate is then limited so that it may be placed at the disposal of those who strongly favor the special interests. The special interests fear that the special privileges which they enjoy, or which they may be seeking to increase, will be taken away or refused if the problems involving the exercise of the privileges and rights belonging to the people should receive proper consideration.

When the Aldrich-Vreeland Emergency Currency Bill was sprung on the House in its finished draft and ready for action to be taken, the debate was limited to three hours and

Banker Vreeland placed in charge. It took so long for copies of the bill to be gotten that many members were unable to secure a copy until within a few minutes of the time to vote. No member who wished to present the people's side of the case was given sufficient time to enable him to properly analyze the bill. I asked for time and was told that if I would vote for the bill it would be given to me, but not otherwise. Others were treated in the same way.

Accordingly, on June 30, 1908, the Money Trust won the first fight and the Aldrich-Vreeland Emergency Law was placed on the statute books. Thus the first precedent was established for the people's guarantee of the rich man's watered securities, by making them a basis on which to issue currency. It was the entering wedge. We had already guaranteed the rich men's money, and now, by this act, the way was opened, and it was intended that we should guarantee their watered stocks and bonds. Of course, they were too keen to attempt to complete, in a single act, such an enormous steal as it would have been if they had included all they hoped ultimately to secure. They knew that they would be caught at it if they did, and so it was planned that the whole thing should be done by a succession of acts. The first three have taken place.

Act No. 1 was the manufacture, between 1896 and 1907, through stock gambling, speculation and other devious methods and devices, of tens of billions of watered stocks, bonds, and securities.

Act No. 2 was the panic of 1907, by which those not favorable to the Money Trust could be squeezed out of business and the people frightened into demanding changes in the banking and currency laws which the Money Trust would frame.

Act No. 3 was the passage of the Aldrich-Vreeland Emergency Currency Bill, by which the Money Trust interests should have the privilege of securing from the Government currency on their watered bonds and securities. But while the act contained no authority to change the form of the bank notes, the U. S. Treasurer (in some way that I have been unable to find a reason for) implied authority and changed the form of bank notes which were issued for the banks on government bonds. These notes had hitherto had printed on them, "This note is secured by bonds of the United States." He changed it to read as follows: "This note is secured by bonds of the United States or other securities." "Or other securities" is the addition that was secured by the special interests. The infinite care the Money Trust exercises in regard to important detail work is easily seen in this piece of management. By that change it was enabled to have the form of the money issued in its favor on watered bonds and securities, the same as bank notes secured on government bonds, and, as a result, the people do not know whether they get one or the other. None of the $500,000,000 printed and lying in the U. S. Treasury ready to float on watered bonds and securities has yet (April, 1913) been used. But it is there, maintained at a public charge, as a guarantee to the Money Trust that it may use it in case it crowds speculation beyond the point of its control. The banks may take it to prevent their own failures, but there is not even so much as a suggestion that it may be used to help keep the industries of the people in a state of prosperity.

The main thing, however, that the Money Trust accomplished as a result of the passing of this act was the appointment of the National Monetary Commission, the membership of which was chiefly made up of bankers, their agents and attorneys, who have generally been educated in favor of, and to have a community of interest with, the Money Trust. The National Monetary Commission was placed in charge of the same Senator Nelson W. Aldrich and Congressman Edward B. Vreeland, who respectively had charge in the Senate and House during the passage of the act creating it.

The act authorized this commission to spend money without stint or account. It spent over $300,000 in order to learn how to form a plan by which to create a greater money trust, and it afterwards recommended Congress to give this proposed trust a fifty-year charter by means of which it could rob and plunder all humanity. A bill for that purpose was introduced by members of the Monetary Commission, and its passage was planned to be the fourth and final act of the campaign to completely enslave the people.

The fourth act, however, is in process of incubation only, and it is hoped that by this time we realize the danger that all of us are in, for it is the final proposed legislation which, if it succeeds, will place us in the complete control of the moneyed interests. History records nothing so dramatic in design, nor so skillfully manipulated, as this attempt to create the National Reserve Association,—otherwise called the Aldrich Plan,—and no fact nor occurrence contemplated for the gaining of selfish ends is recorded in the world's records which equals the beguiling methods of this colossal undertaking. Men, women, and children have been equally unconscious of how stealthily this greatest of all giant octopuses,—a greater Money Trust,—is reaching out its tentacles in its efforts to bind all humanity in perpetual servitude to the greedy will of this monster.

I was in Congress when the panic of 1907 occurred, but I had previously familiarized myself with many of the ways of high financiers. As a result of what I discovered in that study, I set out to expose the Money Trust, the world's greatest financial giant. I knew that I could not succeed unless I could bring public sentiment to my aid. I had to secure that or fail. The Money Trust had laid its plans long before and was already executing them. It was then, and still

is, training the people themselves to demand
the enactment of the Aldrich Bill or a bill similar in effect. Hundreds of thousands of dollars had already been spent and millions were
reserved to be used in the attempt to bring
about a condition of public mind that would
cause demand of the passage of the bill. If no
other method succeeded, it was planned to bring
on a violent panic and to rush the bill through
during the distress which would result from
the panic. It was figured that the people would
demand new banking and currency laws; that it
would be impossible for them to get a definitely
practical plan before Congress when they were
in an excited state and that, as a result, the
Aldrich plan would slip safely through. It was
designed to pass that bill in the fall of 1911 or
1912.

At that time the people had been hearing of
all kinds of trusts but one. Other trusts were
being prosecuted in tne hope of keeping our attention from that one. I had studied the ways
of the trusts and the manner of their organization. I had concluded that they were all the
offspring of one colossal trust, and that particular trust had not been named, but that it was

the trust that desired to pass the Aldrich Bill.
Further, I concluded that if the public could be
advised of that trust, it (the trust) would be
kept so busy defending itself that it would be
compelled to postpone its attempt to force the
passage of the Aldrich Plan by means of the
drastic process of a panic, and that it might
possibly be entirely defeated. Accordingly, I
introduced a resolution naming the Money
Trust and asked for a committee to investigate.

My purpose was accomplished. The Aldrich
Plan was defeated for the time being by the influence of a positive public sentiment which
developed to greater and greater proportions
as I pressed the inquiry, and the press published articles about it. The advocates of the
plan began to look for a means of retreat, and
later they declared the plan abandoned, but lest
that declaration be misconstrued, let us not
deceive ourselves by believing that the purposes
of the Aldrich Plan have been abandoned. They
have not, and the same interests that were advocating the plan are covertly operating in order
to secure a plan that will accomplish the same
results and satisfy the same selfish purposes.

The Aldrich Plan is not dead, but is being advocated under a disguise.

It now becomes important to know what good the investigation of the Money Trust has done when the purposes for which I started the proceedings were accomplished before the resolution even passed. We have previously seen the methods by means of which my resolution was sidetracked by the bosses, and the appointment of a special committee which would honestly go to the root of the evils avoided. If the Money Trust was to hold its sway it must have bankers in charge of the investigation. Let us inquire into the interest that the bankers have heretofore taken in the financial acts of Congress.

The bankers and the money loaners have always framed the financial legislation in their own interests. They have found, from time to time, that they did not anticipate even the extent of their own avarice. The development of new inventions which they could not anticipate has left them at times without quite as complete a control as they insist upon having, and they have kept coming to their subservient Congressmen again and again for more special favors, but since Congress has given them committees of their own in both the Senate and House, and left that class of legislation exclusively to them (to report bills on), they have had things practically their own way. I shall not go over the whole history of their scheme. A recital of a few of their acts will serve to illustrate their method. All we seek to acquire by this study is an understanding of the system, and after that each may make his research as thorough as he chooses. I shall not give the most flagrant cases of which I have knowledge because I am not seeking to stir up strife and hatred for the bankers. I merely think they ought to occupy the same standing in the social order that the rest of us occupy. As a matter of fact, they cannot even get out of their own position until we help them. We have given them so much power and privilege that they cannot handle it, and still they seek more, and they themselves do not know where the trouble lies. The kings of the game do, but the rank and file of their followers do not.

Yes, these money lenders began early to acquire control. They have never let it go. They started in Europe long, long ago, and just as soon as there was anything doing over here they

were on hand. Alexander Hamilton was one of
their supporters. I shall not review his acts, but
shall refer to a few later things emanating
directly from the banks. The English money
lenders have co-operated with those of our
country, and in 1862 an agent, quietly and under
a sort of confidential seal, distributed among
the aristocrats and the wealthy class a circular.
It was called the Hazard Circular and related
in a way to the Civil War. It read:

Quotation "B."

"Slavery is likely to be abolished by the war power
and all chattel slavery abolished. This I and my
European friends are in favor of, for slavery is but
the owning of labor and carries with it the care of
the laborers while the European plan, led on by England, is that capital shall control labor by controlling wages. The great debt that capitalists will
see to it is made out of the war, must be used as a
means to control the volume of money. To accomplish this the bonds must be used as a banking basis.
We are now waiting for the Secretary of the Treasury to make this recommendation to Congress. It
will not do to allow the greenback, as it is called, to
circulate as money any length of time, as we cannot
control that. But we can control the bonds and
through them the bank issues."

This shows how mercenary these usurers are.
Rather than assume the care of the slaves, they
would control labor with the use of capital. It
necessarily followed that when the laborer

ceased to be of service because of sickness or old age, he would be of no concern to capital. He could either get well or die without the capitalists being obliged to provide medical attention or bury the dead. Such was the interest that capital had in the result of the Civil War. The people of this country poured out both their treasure and their blood to establish the political and industrial independence of humanity, and the mercenary capitalists turned a trick of finance and converted the enormous sacrifice made by the people during that struggle into a victory for capital, in order that they might enforce upon humanity the industrial slavery that the trusts preferred rather than the chattel slavery which then existed in the Southern States.

About the close of the war, 1865, we have another example worthy of note. Mr. Jay Cooke, the fiscal agent for the Government, who acted in the interest of the money loaners and bankers of our country and of Europe, published a circular and in it stated, among other things:

Quotation "C."
"We lay down the proposition that our national

debt made permanent and rightly managed, will be a national blessing. The funded debt of the United States is the addition of three thousand millions of dollars to the previously realized wealth of the nation. It is three thousand millions added to the actual available capital."

Did you ever know of a person who thought that his home was worth more to him with a mortgage on it than it would be without? According to Mr. Cooke, it would be. With truthfulness he could have added that the national debt was so much on which to tax the daily earnings of those who survived the horrors of a civil war. He said practically that in another clause of his circular which runs as follows:

"To tax this debt would be to extinguish the capital and lose the wealth."

Is it any wonder that the cost of living is high, and still getting higher, when we have such statesmen to administer our government?

Again in 1877 a circular was issued by authority of the Associated Bankers of New York, Philadelphia, and Boston. It was signed by one James Buel, Secretary, and sent out from 247 Broadway, New York. It was sent to the bankers in all of the States. It read:

Quotation "D."

"Dear Sir:—It is advisable to do all in your power to sustain such prominent daily and weekly newspapers, especially the agricultural and religious press, as will oppose the greenback issue of paper money; and that you also withhold patronage from all applicants who are not willing to oppose the government issue of money. Let the Government issue the coin and the banks issue the paper money of the country, for then we can better protect each other. To repeal the act creating bank notes, or to restore to circulation the government issue of money, will be to provide the people with money and will therefore seriously affect our individual profits as bankers and lenders. See your Congressman at once and engage him to support our interests, that we may control legislation."

Isn't it astounding how very like the bankers of the present time those bankers of 1877 were? Some of them are still with us. "Withhold patronage from all applicants who are not willing to oppose the government issue of money." That was their decree. Again note how they would control the press by sustaining the press, especially the "agricultural and religious press," if these would support the money loaners, but "withhold patronage" if they would not. And note also how they were to "See your Congressman and engage him." Every cunning device was to be used to prevent the people from having the government issue money and to force them to have bank money supported by the government. What simpletons we plain folks have been to pay these bankers for the credit given to them by our own government at our own expense.

I call attention to another of their schemes. This bears a somewhat later date, one which I myself remember. I read the "Panic Circular of 1893" at the time of its issue. It was that circular which started me to studying the problems of finance. The circular was issued direct by The American Bankers' Association, an organization in which most bankers hold membership. It bears the date March 11, 1893, and was sent to the trusted national banks in all states. It read:

Quotation "E."
"Dear Sir:—The interest of national banks requires immediate financial legislation by Congress. Silver, silver certificates and treasury notes must be retired and national bank notes upon a gold basis made the only money. This will require the authorization of five hundred millions to one thousand millions of new bonds as the basis of circulation. You will at once retire one-third of your circulation and call in one-half of your loans. Be careful to make a monetary stringency among your patrons, especially among influential business men. Advocate an extra session of Congress to repeal the purchasing clause of the Sherman law and act with

other banks of your city in securing a large petition
to Congress for its unconditional repeal, per accompanying form.   Use personal influence with your
Congressman, and particularly let your wishes be
known to your Senators.   The future life of national
banks, as fixed and safe investments, depends upon
immediate action, as there is an increasing sentiment
in favor of government legal tender notes and silver
coinage."

One would think that after the bankers had
fooled us so many times, squeezed us by suddenly retiring a part of their circulation, made
the borrowing public pay half their loans, and
brought stringencies among their patrons, that
they would have had things fixed ''for good and
all.''   But no!   They are after us again with
another scheme cleverly disguised.   This time
it is called the Aldrich plan.   Let us compare
the present scheme with those of the past and
note what we find.

Wall Streeters organized the National Citizens' League of Chicago by means of their
secret agents and afterwards that league,
through its secret agents, organized Citizens
Leagues in practically all of the states.   The
purpose for which they were designed was that
they might serve the same purpose with relation
to the present proposed financial legislation

that the Panic Circular of 1893 filled with regard to the legislation then desired by the interests. The circular proposed a "large petition" to be secured through the influence of "influential business men" by forcing a "monetary stringency." This last scheme gets at the Senators and Congressmen in a more persuasive manner than the petitions did. It is also a cunning design by means of which to deceive the people who have become too intelligent to be deceived by the methods formerly practiced.

No one familiar with the facts, and not prejudiced in the matter, doubts for a moment that the National Citizens League of Chicago was an emanation from, and is supported in the main by, Wall Streeters and their dependents. All of the branch leagues throughout the different states are mainly supported from the same source. The leagues invite all people to join, and advertise that by paying $1 admission fee they will be entitled to all of the literature. The receipts from that source have not paid a twentieth part of the expense. But the scheme gets the people to join, and the greatest number of those who do join do not know from what source the league gets its principal support. One of its principal definite purposes is to publish a financial journal called "Banking Reform," the purpose of which is to influence us and cause us to ask our Congressman to support some money plan that has (covertly) received Wall Street's approval.

This money and banking business is of great importance. A study of the principles and methods by which it is conducted requires so much time and energy, because of its immensity, that comparatively few people have any chance to give it a thorough study. That is why the so-called Citizens Leagues, organized by the influence of Wall Street, have been able to induce some honest men to join in the advocacy of its plans. The leagues claim that they are not prejudiced in favor of, nor against any plan, but wish to consider all and choose the best— a very beguiling method, is it not? But the literature alone, which is, by the way, supplied by the Wall Streeters, and distributed by the leagues, is proof enough for anyone who wishes to know the truth.

The method used by the Citizens Leagues is simply a change made from the old method of direct action used by the money loaners, namely, petitions and letters induced by "creating a monetary stringency." The people are better educated now, and it requires a more subtle game to fool them, and a more round-about way is selected by the interests, in order that they may conceal their underground work. I have had occasion to investigate the origin of the National Citizens' League, the father of them all, and since we shall hear more of its work in its attempts to foster on us a further tenure of the money loaners' control of our life's action, I wish to insert a part of a speech I made in Congress on the plan it advocated. It is as follows:

"The subtle and underground influence of Wall Street in furthering and advocating that plan is illustrated in the formation of the National Citizens' League.

"It would be interesting to inquire why no other such powerful citizens leagues are formed to advocate other important problems than this Aldrich Plan. . . . I might run through a long list of problems, vastly important to the people, and yet not one, except this Aldrich Plan, has been dignified by the formation of national citizens leagues with branches in forty-four states. Is it because the people are, by the Aldrich Plan, to give billions of dollars to a private monopoly that these leagues have been formed? Draw your own inference. Certain interests got busy inspiring citizens leagues. I believe in citizens leagues, but I would like to see them started voluntarily by the people themselves. I do not believe in a few men getting together and appointing themselves to the offices of a so-called citizens league and then solicit citizens to join simply to say 'Amen.'

"The chief officials of the leagues had a conference and luncheon at the Great Northern Hotel, Chicago. It was attended by the officials of the branch organizations. Its president, John V. Farwell, in opening the meeting, stated:

Quotation "F."

" 'The National Citizens' League, with organizations in forty-four states of the Union, with its members drawn from all our agricultural, manufacturing and mercantile interests, is the strongest organization of its kind ever enlisted in a great public service.'

" 'We do not advocate any bill now before Congress,' stated Mr. Farwell. In the next breath he disregarded his solemn statement that, 'We de not advocate any bill now before Congress,' and he advocated the Aldrich Bill, which was then and is now before Congress. This is the same bill that I am discussing. He spoke as follows:

Quotation "G."

" 'We do, however, recognize in the report that has been unanimously made by the National Monetary Commission the greatest step that has yet been taken in this country to give us a sound banking system. We believe that this report embodies those fundamental principles for which we all stand. The report is a conscientious, painstaking effort to provide a working basis for legislation in Congress. We will continue to advocate these principles, confident that Congress will give us the legislation the country demands.'

"How could the National Citizens' League indorse and advocate the bill more subtly than in the language of that speech? Not only did it advocate the plan at its meeting but it employed speakers to travel all over the country and speak in its favor. It distributed all kinds of literature in support of the Aldrich bill, and as far as practicable for it to do so, it suppressed all literature that opposed that plan. Wall Street is the underground support of the leagues, and Wall Street sought through the help of the leagues to force Congress to pass the Aldrich bill before the general public had solved its mysteries because it knew that once the public learned the real purpose of the bill it would not permit its passage. Members of the leagues, with few exceptions, do not know at present that they are advocating the Wall Street plan."

"I particularly call attention to one phase of the Wall Street underground work. I have

already received letters on this particular phase
of the subject from over one hundred different
banks in many different States Only seven of
these letters are from my own State. The letters written by the New York banks to their
correspondents are all practically the same. I
shall quote one set only, as an example of what
they all are. To wit:

Quotation "H."

"'The Chase National Bank,
"'New York, Feb. 21, '1912.

"'Gentlemen:—We inclose a letter from the National Citizens' League which we have been asked to
forward to you. The campaign of education which the
league is conducting in favor of currency and banking reform is non-partisan in character and national
in scope. We believe it of direct importance to the
business interests of the country. The merchants
interested in the work have felt that, while they
regard themselves as responsible for the raising of
funds for the prosecution of the work, the country at
large should know that the banking interest is in
sympathy with the work. Any correspondence
should be taken up with Mr. Isidor Straus, treasurer, Broadway and Thirty-fourth Street, New York,
and any contributions made direct to him.

"'Yours sincerely,
"'A. H. WIGGINS, President.'"

You will notice that the letter does not give
the name of the bank to which it was sent.
Some of these letters are written to others than

bankers. You will realize that it is another case of the Wall Streeters using the interests' method in order to scare the country bankers, merchants and others, and not reap the blame for the "monetary stringency." The following blank was enclosed in the letter of President Wiggins, who is one of the "big six" Wall Street bankers. It was intended that it should be filled out by the bankers to whom it was sent. The blank was:

Quotation "I."

"New York, Feb. ...., 1912.
"To ISIDOR STRAUS, ESQ.,
    "Treasurer National Citizens' League,
        "100 Broad Street, New York City.
    "Dear Sir:—I inclose herewith my check for $...... as my subscription to the fund of the National Citizens' League in its campaign of public education for the promotion of a sound banking system.
        "Yours truly,
        "..................."

Attached to the letter of the Chase National Bank was a letter from which I quote a few paragraphs as follows:

Quotation "J."
"Dear Sir:—You insure your property against fire, your business against risks, yourself against incapacity and death. For this protection you pay many annual premiums of considerable amount.

"We ask you to pay a single premium for the insurance of your business against money panics, against the business collapse that attends them, and the business depression that follows them."

* * * *

"These are the benefits of banking and currency reform. And this reform is assured if the business men will combine and lend it the same support they gave the sound money in the 'nineties.

"The issue is just as live and big. Sound currency needs a sound currency system back of it. Business isn't paralyzed today as it was four years ago. Another panic is not anticipated. But the fact remains and it must be faced squarely now, that under our present defective and dangerous banking system disastrous panics can not be controlled. Revision is demanded—now."

* * * *

"Business men all over the country, irrespective of rank and party lines, have organized the National Citizens' League for the promotion of a sound banking system.'

"The league does not advocate any particular plan, but is carrying on a nation-wide campaign of education in an economical and legitimate way, to the end of arousing Congress to prompt and business-like action free from the prejudice of partisan politics.'

"Any subscription from $1 upward will constitute a membership in the league."

* * * *

"If you count this a good business investment, with 1907 clearly remembered, will you fill out and return the inclosed blank?

"Yours very truly,
"JOHN CLAFLIN,
"President New York State Branch
of the National Citizens' League."

I ask you to re-read the Panic Circular of
1893, Quotation "E." It is important in connection with the above letter.

I have similar letters which were sent out by
the Wall Street banks. These letters were sent
into all of the states. Every banker, except
one, who wrote me, expressly requested that
I should not disclose his name, for to do so,
they wrote, would bring upon them the disfavor
of certain business interests. I shall quote one
of these letters in order to show what I believe
to be the attitude held by the bankers in the
small towns. This belief is suppressed because
the country bankers fear that their business
will be harmed if they incur the disfavor of
the special interests. I omit from the letter
all the facts that would identify the party, for
reasons appearing in the letter itself. It is as
follows:

Quotation "K."
        "................., Minn., 1912.
"Hon. C. A. Lindbergh,
        "Washington, D. C.
    "Dear Sir:—I have noticed with considerable in-
terest your charge against the National Citizens'
League—that it is being financed by Wall Street
influence. I am inclosing herewith a circular letter
from a Wall Street bank, soliciting subscriptions for

the league from the Minnesota banks. This letter
comes from our New York correspondent. I assume
that the plan is to reach our banks in this way
through their New York depository. I take the liberty of sending this to you as it may be of some value
to you in your campaign against the iniquitous
Aldrich currency measure.

"This letter comes to you from a stranger, but
from one who is in hearty sympathy with your congressional work. I would, of course, not want either
my name or bank mentioned publicly in this connection.

"Respectfully,

"...................,

"Vice-President."

It is to be regretted that the conditions are
such that bankers dare not come forward and
openly fight this "iniquitious Aldrich currency
measure," as this man so aptly terms it.

It has been announced that the Aldrich plan
has been abandoned because it is believed that
the name would prove disastrous to its chances
for adoption, but although this attempt has
been made in order to make it appear that the
bill has been abandoned, the substance has
been retained and is still being pushed by the
Wall Streeters for adoption. It is the substance and not the name that is material to us,
and we should center our fight on the substance
and disregard the name with which it is labeled.

The bankers are willing to join with the citizens not selfishly interested, and aid them in their attempt to correct the present system. But they insist that we should show strength enough to make our fight seem to have a reasonable chance of success. They are too practical, and I may as well add selfish, to jeopardize their interests, by embracing a cause that fails to give some reasonable promise of success, and no sound policy favorable to the general welfare has any prospect of success until the people themselves understand the ways and means by which to meet their own vital necessities. Until they do, the temptation to fleece them is too great for the selfish interests to resist.

While I was making an aggressive fight against the Aldrich plan, the National Citizens' League of Chicago sent the Hon. Robert W. Bonynge to its branch league in my own State to make speeches for the Aldrich plan. Mr. Bonynge was himself a member of the National Monetary Commision that reported to Congress on the Aldrich plan. He was sent to my home town, Little Falls, and to two other towns in the district that I represent, to advocate the Aldrich plan. Incidentally it was expected to

influence the people of my own district against
me because I opposed the Aldrich plan. They
hoped by doing so to force me to abandon the
fight.

After Mr. Bonynge completed his lecture
course, which covered several states, he sent
the following notice to Members of Congress:

Quotation "L."

"26 Exchange Place,
"New York City, Dec. 2nd, 1912.
"Robert W. Bonynge, lately of the Colorado Bar,
and Paul Bonynge announce the formation of a
partnership for the general practice of law under the
firm name of
"BONYNGE AND BONYNGE,
"with offices at the above address.
"Telephone 4967 Broad."

The location of 26 Exchange Place, New York
City, is down in the Wall Street district.

Each fact brings out more clearly that there
is an attempt being made to make the greatest steal of all times, but because of its
enormity, and because the people understand
the social problems better, it is necessary that
more adroit measures be resorted to than were
formerly necessary, in order that special legislation may be secured, which will be favorable
to the Money Trust. The National Monetary

Commission was no sooner created than plans were formulated to advocate a scheme that was expected to be evolved by it, and the National Citizens' League of Chicago was put into effective organization for that purpose very soon after the commission was created.

Let us further consider the work of these leagues, because they were organized as agencies by means of which it was expected to fool the people and secure additional favors for the Money Trust. If you will again refer to circulars B, C, D, and E, you will observe the subtleness of the following circular which was issued by the National Citizens' League of Chicago, and distributed by its branch leagues as a means of accomplishing the latest designs of the Money Trust. It reads:

Quotation "M."
"THE NATIONAL CITIZENS' LEAGUE
"For the promotion of a sound banking system,
"223 West Jackson Boulevard,
"Chicago, Ill.
"To the Members of the National Citizens' League:
"There is enclosed herewith for your information a brief report of the progress made by the League during the year which has just closed, a statement of the situation and the prospects ahead. You will observe at once that it was never more important that the work of education be pushed, that discus-

sion of the question be promoted and study of it urged.

"By joining the League you proved your interest in the cause of banking reform. Every member of the League should prove again that interest by doing active missionary work. It is necessary to spread the gospel of a sound, panic-proof banking system.

"President-elect Wilson and dozens of Congressmen have expressed the view that public opinion on this question is still unformed. It is the work of the League to form public opinion and impress the fact on Congressmen.

"One way is for the League members to write direct to their Representatives and Senators, urging action and giving reasons for it. Another is to urge your interested friends to do the same. And another way is for every member of the League to get a new member. You know the returns members receive. You know whether membership is worth while.

"The league has less than 10,000 members now. This number can be doubled before February 1. It will be doubled if every member will get a new member.

"Will you do your share?

"When the League has 100,000 members there will be tangible and audible proof that public opinion is crystallized, sound and militant.

"The members of the League must act with the League and for banking reform.

"Very truly yours,

"A. D. WELTON, General Secretary."

Notice especially, how the letter says, "One way is for League Members to write direct to Representatives and Senators," etc. This is substantially the same old story that we find in quotations "D" and "E." Notice also that the membership of the League is less than 10,000. They have not been able to fool many of the country bankers because most of them realize that the Aldrich plan would make of them merely the agents of Wall Street.

The following shows the method by which the State Leagues assist in upholding the purposes for which the National Citizens' League was formed. Here we have the Minnesota branch of it:

Quotation "N."
"Memorandum by
"President JOHN H. RICH,
"The Citizens' League of Minnesota.
"The publications and report of the Monetary Commission form the most complete and valuable reference library on banking and currency in every civilized country that has ever been gathered together. This was available for the use of the Glass committee when it began its sessions.

"The Glass Committee has been at work since last April and has supplemented the testimony taken by the Monetary Commission by calling many new witnesses. Sufficient testimony has been taken. This subject has been presented from the view point of hundreds of the best business men, financiers and economists in the United States and hearings to take testimony and obtain information have been held (by the Monetary Commission) in the principal commercial centers.

"Since June, 1911, the National Citizens' League and the Minnesota branch, affiliated with it, have been devoting their energies solely to broadening the

public information on this subject. In forty-four
states this work has been energetically going on.
While all business men have not become expert,
very many have become well informed and possess
clearly defined opinions favorable to a reform of the
banking and currency system.

"The press, at first antagonistic, has come to see
the necessity of modernizing American methods and
changing to a sound banking system. In Minnesota
the radical newspapers have greatly modified their
expressions and many of the latter now favor a
reform.

"The Monetary Commission Bill (Aldrich Bill)
cannot pass. The Glass Committee Bill will shortly
be before Congress. The Fowler Bill is before Congress now, and other bills will be introduced. It is
probable that the Glass Bill will be found acceptable
in large part, and the outlook for the enactment of
legislation is very favorable.

"Congress undoubtedly can, if it will, settle this
question at the forthcoming special session. It will
be very undesirable to permit it to go over to the
following long session, because of the danger that
it may be made a political question and enter into
the Congressional elections.

"The influence of business men, exerted at this
time in the form of letters to representatives in Congress, and members of the Senate, will be a powerful
aid in the present movement to secure prompt consideration and action on this question. Your active
co-operation in this respect is earnestly requested."

The secretary of the association inclosed the
Rich statement within a letter of his own to
Mr. Hugh J. Hughes, editor of *"Farm, Stock
and Home,"* an influential publication with a
large circulation. It was as follows:

Quotation "Q."

"Minneapolis, Minn., Jan. 24, 1913.

"HUGH J. HUGHES,
    "Farm, Stock, and Home,
        "Minneapolis, Minn.

"Dear MR. HUGHES:

"The preliminary draft of the Glass Committee Bill will be sent within a few days for the private examination of a selected list of business men, bankers, and economists. This indicates that the Committee, after the hearings it has been conducting, plans to act promptly. The best information available indicates that this bill will be acceptable in large measure.

"The national organization believes that if business men show sufficient interest and will act promptly, it will be possible to secure action on banking and currency reform at the coming special session. Any bill will naturally undergo the modifying influences of debates and hearings in Congress, and if a fairly good measure is reported by the Committee, it will be possible to perfect it before passage.

"Your influence with members of Congress will be of great assistance. In behalf of President Rich, who is absent from the state at present, and the national organization, I am instructed to earnestly request your active co-operation by writing personally to the Members of Congress from this state, and to any in Congress from other states, with whom you are acquainted, urging,

"That Congress act on this subject at the special session.

"That sufficient hearings have been held.

"That the business of the country needs this reform and should have it at once.

"I beg to call your attention to the memorandum by President Rich, attached, and also to the recent

report of the national organization which you may
not have seen.

"We will appreciate it if you will advise us of any
action you take, in order that we may be informed.

"Yours very truly,

CURTIS L. MOSHER, Secretary."

The following is taken from the report of the
National Citizens' League, Chicago:

Quotation "P."

"The League was obliged to get publicity through
other sources. It printed and distributed in the first
six months of 1912 nearly one million pamphlets. It
began the publication of a semi-monthly—now published monthly—news bulletin, and, as interest increased under this system, it prepared hundreds of
newspaper articles."

"The League's text-book, 'Banking Reform,' was
published in May. It was sent free to members of
the League, and about 1500 copies were distributed
to newspapers for review. Nearly 12,000 copies of
the book have been distributed. The circulation of
the news bulletin, 'Banking Reform,' is now 30,000
copies."

The membership of this league is less than
10,000. The fee charged is $1. This fee entitles
the member to all of the literature as long as
the League lasts. The postage account alone
amounts to more than the entire amount of the
membership fee. The amount paid to the lectur-
ers alone is more than the entire fees amount to,
and the other expenses of the League are simply

enormous, but, Wall Streeters are seeking to rob the people of tens of billions of dollars and that makes it worth while for those who expect to secure the benefits to pay the main costs. The Philadelphia bankers contributed over $100,000 to this league's campaign. Everything is being done which it is thought will cause the people to think as these bankers wish them to.

If it were not so important that we should know the truth about this disguise (which the leagues actually are for Wall Street), I would not take the trouble to give so many of these facts, but to know them may save us from having heaped upon us the greatest burden that humanity has yet had to bear. We should beware of the so-called National Citizens' League and its branches. Numerous other facts could be shown that would be sufficient by themselves to convince any impartial person beyond a doubt that these leagues were conceived in the brains of Wall Streeters, officered by men educated in Wall Street methods, and supported by the Wall Street system. It deceives the people, and more especially the agents of the people in Congress, who are entrusted with the people's work and expected to help create a new banking and currency system. Its aim is to aid them in gaining the control of the

financial monetary system in order to further
enslave humanity in the aggregate.

Is it at all strange that the Glass Committee,
composed mostly of bankers, their agents and
attorneys, should be referred to by the Citizens'
League as having given out that "the preliminary draft of the Glass Bill" would "be sent
in a few days for the private examination of
a selected list of business men, bankers, and
economists." Oh, what inconsistency! The
Citizens Leagues, themselves, pretending to be
organized for "publicity," sending out a preliminary draft for the *private* examination of
a *selected list* of business men, bankers and
economists. What about the farmer, the wage
earner, and people generally? It is the same
old game of deception. The people are always
the last to know anything that is planned by
the interests in order that they may only "lock
their doors when their goods have been stolen."

I wrote to the Glass Committee for a copy of
its draft for a banking and currency plan and
three weeks later received the following answer:

Quotation "Q."
                                "February 12, 1913.
"Hon. C. A. LINDBERGH,
    "House of Representatives.
"My Dear Mr. LINDBERGH:
    "I have been so engrossed recently with commit-

tee work that I have been unable to give attention to
my correspondence, which accounts for this belated
response to your letter of recent date.   Replying
now, I beg to say that we have not yet formulated a
currency bill, but just as soon as we shall have done
so, I will be glad to let you have one of the first
copies of the measure.

   "With cordial regards,

               "Sincerely yours,

                      "CARTER GLASS."

It was the duty of the Glass Committee to
first report to Congress, but no effort has thus
far, April, 1913, been made by that Committee
to make such a report or to furnish Congress
with a preliminary draft of a bill, and when
the Citizens' League had sent out their letter
to the "selected list" informing them that the
preliminary draft of the Glass Committee bill
would be sent out in a few days for the examination of a "selected list of bankers,
economists, business men," etc., Congress had
heard nothing about it.   Many Members requested the preliminary draft, but it was impossible to secure even a suggestion about it.
I expressly requested it because I wished to
read it and because of the many requests I received from people who were trying to keep
posted, but the committee furnished me with
no information other than the letter written by

Mr. Glass, its chairman. It is now four months since the Citizens' League promised "in a few days" to send to its selected list of bankers and economists the draft of the Glass Bill, but the public has not been permitted up to this time to see it. Further, the Wall Streeters, as might be expected, steered the persons whom they desired to appear before that Committee in order to influence, insofar as it would be possible, the form of any proposed bill. The real producers and consumers of the country and those who have studied their needs the most have had no hearing before that committee. Those who have been allowed to testify are principally those whose business it is to get all they can out of the people.

It will be observed that the letter written by Mr. Glass was dated 19 days later than the letter written by the Secretary of the Minnesota Citizens' League to Mr. Hugh J. Hughes. The Secretary of that League stated on Jan. 24th that the preliminary draft of the Glass Committee bill would be sent within a few days for the "private examination of a selected list of business men, bankers, and economists." Mr. Glass' reply to me states that his committee "have not yet formulated a currency bill." It will be noticed that he makes no suggestion as to when one will be formulated, nor does he say anything about a preliminary draft.

Now, then, note what *"Banking Reform,"* the publication of the National Citizens' League, said in its issue of February 1st, 1913. On the front cover, surrounded by a heavy black line, is the following:

Quotation "R."
    "Do BUSINESS MEN WANT BANKING REFORM?
    "Speaking before the Chamber of Commerce of the United States in Washington, January 21, Congressman Glass, of the Banking and Currency Committee, said that upon the business and commercial men of the country rests a large part of the responsibility for action on remedial banking legislation. He gave warning that unless the business world acts promptly, there would be a long postponement of currency legislation."

On the same cover, immediately following, is a notice to members of the League in the following form:

Quotation "S."
"To Members of the National Citizens' League:
    "Congress is wavering over the question of banking reform. The Democratic leaders are undecided whether to bring in a currency bill at the special session in the Spring or defer action until the regular session next December.
    "The reason given for this hesitation is that the

business men of the country have not made it plain to Congress that they demand a new banking law. In short, business men have been challenged to show that there is a demand for immediate action.

"There is such a demand.

"The one thing to do is to get it home to Congress that demand exists. The only way to do that is to tell your representatives and senators that you want immediate action.

"If business men and bankers of the country make it clear to Congress that immediate action is demanded, there will be action at the special session.

"Through Representative Glass, of the Banking and Currency Committee, Congress has said to the business men of the country that unless they act promptly the remedial legislation 'so badly needed will be long deferred.'

"The question has been placed squarely before the business men of the country.

"Make your decision.

"Write a letter to your representative. Write to your senator. Write to Mr. Glass. Write to Mr. Underwood.

"President-elect Wilson has been quoted as holding the view that public sentiment as to banking reform has not yet crystallized. Write to Mr. Wilson, if you know him. If you don't know him, it is a good way to get acquainted."

Following these disclosures by the National Citizens' League, comes its April issue of *"Banking Reform"* with the following notice:

"LAUGHLIN RETIRES.

"J. Laurence Laughlin, Chairman of the Executive Committee of the National Citizens' League since its organization, has returned to his position as professor of political economy in the University of Chicago.

"In June, 1911, Professor Laughlin was given a year's leave from the university, that he might give all his time to the campaign of education undertaken by the League. Last fall this leave was extended for three months, and then until April 1st, at the request of the League's directors.

"To the League Professor Laughlin brought, in addition to natural endowments of an unusual nature and a profound knowledge of economics, a wide experience in campaigns for sound money and better banking conditions. On all the questions involved in the campaign he was able to speak with authority. He has worked indefatigably, and it is largely due to his efforts and his persistence that the campaign enters the final stage with flattering prospects of a successful outcome. . . ."

The reader knows that the University of Chicago is an institution endowed by John D. Rockefeller, with nearly $50,000,000. It may truly be said to be the Rockefeller University. Of course it does not follow that its professors would teach as Rockefeller wished them to, nor that there is any understanding between him and them. They may be, and undoubtedly in most cases are, independent in their work, but in the selection of the professors for that institution careful consideration has always been given to select such as actually believe in the general scheme of things as they have developed under the present capitalistic era.

In the same issue of *Banking Reform* was an article from which I quote the following parts:

"While this was going on [referring to the investigation of the Money Trust] another section of the Banking and Currency Committee was doing effective work. This section, presided over by Representative Carter Glass, who will be Chairman of the Banking and Currency Committee in the 63rd Congress, has given nearly a year to study. It has held many hearings at which bankers and business men gave information and opinions. It has had expert counsel. It has had the benefit of all the work done by the Monetary Commission. It has digested the information, reached a conclusion and has a plan of reform practically outlined.

"There are some new actors on the scene, however. There is a new President, a new Secretary of the Treasury, and a new Chairman of a new Banking and Currency Committee in the new Senate. We need not worry about the President. He is too familiar with economic questions to admit doubt of his power to grasp the details of any plan of banking reform instantly. The Secretary of the Treasury is well equipped to come to a speedy conclusion, and Senator Owen, who has not yet had time to familiarize himself with details, has long been a banker and will have the advantage of the work of his associates."

Senator Owen, as the reader probably knows, is the chairman of the Banking and Currency Committee in the Senate. It is wonderful what absolute information the National Citizens' League claims to have as to what will happen in Congress. The committees that control

financial legislation in both the Senate and
House are presided over by chairmen who are
bankers and personally are financially interested in the proposed legislation. The people
of this country have good reason to be ashamed
of their Congress for permitting such a state
of affairs, but it is not only the chairmen who
preside who are thus interested. These committees are chiefly composed of bankers, their
agents and attorneys, all of whom have a personal financial interest.

We do not expect the National Citizens'
League to admit that it is a creature of Wall
Street. We know that it repudiates Wall Street
on the same principle that all things of that
character are denied by those who join in them.
We know, of course, that in promoting the formation of the State leagues, everything possible
was done to conceal its Wall Street affiliations.
We know that that method enabled it to secure
many members who are opposed to the Wall
Street demands. But after all, its admission
of having only 10,000 members, after its statement of having sent out in the first six months
nearly a million pamphlets, is sufficient to show
that the 94,000,000 people are not falling over

each other in their eagerness to be gathered in by this Wall Street scheme. And it will also be borne in mind that of the 10,000 members that it has secured in its several years of existence, some were always Wall Street supporters, or those employed by or under the domination of Wall Streeters; that they are active for selfish reasons, and therefore will follow the suggestion made by the Panic Circular of 1893: That is, to "Use personal influence with your Congressman and particularly let your wishes be known to your Senator."

Thousands of letters asking immediate financial legislation are now pouring in on Members of Congress. Some are written in good faith with the honest hope of influencing Congressmen in favor of just legislation. But the majority of the letters received are from persons selfishly interested, while those who are not selfishly interested seldom take the trouble to write. And yet, it is the duty of every citizen to take an interest in this most important subject and write to his Congressman and I do not criticize those who write, whether their purpose is a selfish or unselfish one. The vast majority of citizens should have a similar in-

terest in this proposed legislation; an interest
which is worth their most earnest thought and
consideration, and their influence in shaping
the proposed legislation. To all of these I suggest that they should write to their Congressmen on all problems of vital importance requiring the action of Congress, and then it will
not appear to the Congressmen that the interest
of the public is only in shaping legislation that
will further promote the special interests.

The Congressmen receive a dozen and more
letters from those selfishly interested to every
one that they receive from the general public
whose interest it is simply to preserve the general welfare.

Having defined what I am convinced to have
been the original and controlling influence in
the organization of the so-called National
Citizens' League and its State branches, I do
not wish to dismiss the subject and leave the
impression that its members generally desire
to fasten on the country a false money system,
but I do not hesitate in saying that those who
control the distribution of literature do so in
the interests of the selfish Wall Streeters, but
there is no disposition on my part to make the

public believe that these men are wilfully opposed to the public welfare. They are a production of this capitalistic era and they believe in it and are fighting for its supremacy, but as against that, I claim that no careful honest student will deny that the commercialism and speculation of the present period, and the basis on which business and speculation are conducted, lead the rank and file of the population into industrial slavery—in fact that condition actually exists, now, and it is that that I am pointing out, and trying to remedy.

INTEREST, DIVIDENDS AND RENTS.

The greatest of all the present social burdens is the excessive interest, dividends and rent charges levied on us by those who control centralized capital. It may seem to those possessing great wealth that they are vested with the right to levy for its use whatever toll they please upon the plain people. What they do levy makes it evident that they think the people owe them more than it is possible for us to pay.

I shall not question the present extent of the individual ownership of capital, even though I might do so (in a degree) considering the present methods of obtaining it. But I do now question the methods of its present use. I concede that everyone has a right to the products of his energy, properly applied, and also to a reasonable compensation for the same, but, I deny that anyone has any right to prevent such an organization of society as will prohibit those who possess the present wealth of the world from charging for its use a toll that is measured by monopoly regulation, and increased more and more as the necessity of the people increases, and the grasp of the monopolies tightens into a strangle-hold.

The mental and physical need of a people is a condition of their existence and not a matter of production or limitation, to be subject to the prey of individuals, and as the things necessary to supply their needs are constantly in demand, their cost to consumers should be determined by the expense of production, and not by the opportunity presented for taking an unfair advantage of an inherent condition. Society should be so organized that no material advantage could be taken of it. My objection to capital as a power is not so much based upon what capital now costs, as it is upon the claim of the capitalists that they have the right or power which justifies their attempt to control society and not permit it to become independent of capital. Capitalists could not exist as such, if society—the Government of the people did not make it possible. It is ridiculous for the capitalists to claim the right to strangle and impoverish the very people who make the ownership and value of capital possible. Such a claim is not to be justified under any pretense. I am determined to show that the people could be

absolutely independent of the capitalists if they
would make use of their own social advantages,
and that capital would then be wholly employed
on terms of usefulness, instead of forming the
basis for all sorts of extortion, as is now the
case. We can so reconstruct society that it will
be self-perpetuating instead of as now, self-
exhaustive.

Everyone should realize that it is not possible
for us to secure absolute justice in all practical
dealings, and that there will be more or less inequality under any condition that man can
establish. But that fact does not justify our
support of practices that, by their natural application, make a few men immensely wealthy,
create many parasites, and make industrial
slaves of the masses. Our present system does
all of that by its very nature. By that I mean
that the law as it now stands and is interpreted
by the courts and legislatures, forces that condition upon us and the manner in which commerce and speculation go on forces the people
into unfavorable conditions even more rapidly
than if the letter of the law were followed.

Government is properly the framing of rules
of conduct that aid in rendering the results of

transactions entered into by the people more advantageous, and not in fostering monopolies as it now does. But the present social belief seems to be that Government should support the capitalists in the collection of interest, dividends, and rent charges which are so excessive that they cannot be collected except by an excessive reduction of the compensation made to those rendering useful services, and increasing the hours of labor for the producers. The use of this false system is undermining the strength of our nation and will ultimately destroy it, unless we substitute a true economic one. If interest, dividends, and rents were based on the economic savings of those to whom they are paid, or on capital acquired in a just and proper manner, there would be no dangerous accumulation. A few do save and secure interest on some part of their actual earnings, but the general public does not save anything on which to collect either interest or dividends.

It does not seem credible that the farmer, the wage earner, and others should continue to perform useful services, when they know (at the same time) that that part of the product which is the result of their work, but in excess of their pay, and a proper compensation to the employer, forms dead capital on which they and their children will be taxed in the future by a geometrical progression of accumulated profits which will add to their daily burdens and force them and their children to continue living a life of poverty. Does it seem possible that such a condition is supported by the laws of our land and the decrees of our courts? Look at the great combinations of wealth, commonly known as trusts. They are the logical effects of the geometrical progression of interest, dividends and rents, all of which result in a greater and greater centralization of material wealth to be possessed by those same trusts. They are our masters now by virtue of the practice of that rule, and will continue to be so just as long as we allow the present practices to continue. They are the fruits resulting from the peoples toil and accumulated by the wealth absorbers who, by the rules of government and practice in business, possess the privilege of taxing all of the people. It is virtually the same system that prevails in England. In 1822 the land in England was owned by 165,000 people. One-half of the land in the whole kingdom is now owned by less than fifteen persons. Less than a dozen persons in our own country dominate its finances. It is easy to understand how that is possible if one seeks carefully to get a correct understanding of the rules by which society is governed.

How does it happen that the legislatures and the courts have the right to measure the services—that is, the use of dead property—with a more important scale than it measures the services of living persons? It is not because of dishonesty, but it is because the legislatures and the judges, who are men like ourselves, have failed lamentably to see whither we would be carried by such doctrines. But the light of a new day has broken, and the meaning is clear. Who shall say that, understanding, we will permit the practice to go on indefinitely? Who will deny our right to protect ourselves from such a system? We absolutely know that no people can (on the past and present basis) produce so-called capital and centralize it in individual ownership, along with the right of the owners to tax us by the rule of geometrical progression of accumulative interest, dividends, and rents, without making of us a nation of insolvents and creating a condition of poverty for all men. Most men are in a condition of poverty now. Also, we absolutely know that the trusts, as a result of the centralizing of the control of the industrial agencies and material resources, operated in connection with their juggling of credits and money, have made us dependent upon the trusts for employment. This is the industrial slavery that the capitalistic interests prefer to chattel slavery. If we were chattel slaves they would have to care for us in sickness and old age, whereas now they are not concerned with us except for the time during which we work for them.

Knowing these facts, will the people continue to remain in such a state of bondage? Certainly not! The trusts have taught us the principle of combination. If it is good and profitable for the trusts, it is good and profitable for the people. It would be better to have one great trust created by all of the people for their common benefit than to have our actions controlled by several trusts operated for the individual benefit of a few persons. We must make a choice and either accept absolute Socialism or establish Individualism with opportunity for all. For one or the other we are bound to stand, or we shall all fall.

THE CAPITALISTS DEMAND A SOCIALISM OF DOLLARS, THEY TO OWN THEM—IN OTHER WORDS, A MONEY TRUST, AND THEREFORE THEY ARE OPPOSED TO THE PEOPLE BECOMING SOCIALISTS IN THEIR OWN RIGHT. The trusts will maintain the first and prevent the latter if they can do so. Let us understand this clearly. The capitalists all denounce the existence of socialistic tendencies of whatever kind, if they are held by the majority of the people. But they are socialists themselves, as their absolute control of concentrated capital will show. They form combinations and operate them for their joint advantage. Yes, that is socialism operated in the interests of the selected few. Socialism for them means their absolute control of the material products resulting from the toil of the people,—the right to charge for the use of this material and to make of us industrial slaves. They are practical socialists in the interests of the few. But, they are filled with shivering horrors when the people suggest the practice of socialism by themselves, for themselves.

Would it not be more desirable and much more practical for the general welfare of the people to have socialism include all of us than it is to permit the trusts to adopt and practice a form of socialism for themselves alone? Notwithstanding that, I do not advocate socialism in the entire sense in which that term is commonly understood. Ordinarily, one can attend to his own affairs with less waste to himself than there would be if his business was everybody's business. I believe that the individual can do his own life work, and secure his fortune, better than the state could do it for him, provided that the state had reasonable laws and regulations to govern in the interests of all the people. I believe that with the human brain, and the inclinations of the people generally as we find them now, we can be assured of greater progress under the influence of individual incentive than would be probable if property were made a common stock held in trust for all. Theoretically, socialism is beautiful. Theoretically I believe in it, and I would prefer that it should be in actual operation rather than that the present methods of commerce, business, and general practices should continue.

No one doubts that socialism will take the place of the trusts and other selfish organizations now existing if we do not adopt methods by which the people generally shall be able to reap more benefit from their own well-directed energies. The Socialists are seeking to give better results to humanity as a whole, and if that can be accomplished through the establishment of socialism more satisfactorily than by any other system, the Socialists certainly ought to win. We cannot continue to allow the mental and physical state of society to be the basis on which are issued the stocks, bonds, and other securities for which we are taxed. That is, we cannot permit our good will, our inclinations, and desires, nor our dire necessities to be taken advantage of for the purpose of selfish promotion in stocks, bonds and securities.

The one objection most commonly heard in opposition to socialism is that too many persons would shirk their duties, and that others who were active and willing would be forced to do more work than it was their duty to perform. That cannot be urged as a legitimate objection and sufficient to cause us to reject Socialism in favor of our present system, because under the

present system there are more idlers, and
others who are supported by the sweat of
others' toil, than could possibly exist under any
other system, unless we were to accept a state
of anarchy which would require no system at
all.   But we now have a worse affliction than
idlers. We have the greedy trusts, and they are
operating under conditions that enable them to
appropriate the products of our industry and
create wealth which is concentrated into the
hands of a few who not only levy a most bur-
densome toll on the present generation, but possess the legal privilege and, apparently, the
opportunity to enforce the same conditions
upon future generations. The idlers die and
cease to be a further burden, but it is not so
with the trusts. They continue. The remedy
for our social evils does not consist so much in
changing the system of government as it does
in increasing the general intelligence of the
people so that they may learn how to govern.

The only excuse for government is the facility
it affords the citizens for securing advantages
that operate for the common welfare, which
could not be obtained with the same degree of
equability   through   independent   individual

action. In no case has government so signally neglected its function as in its failure to issue money and control the charges made for its use. Banks and individuals have been permitted to set up a system for financial action which is supported by credits and the products of the people's industries. Through its use they are enabled to collect exorbitant dividends, interest, and profits on what they do not produce.

From the testimony given by George F. Baker (President of the First National Bank of New York City) before the committee appointed to investigate the Money Trust, we learn that the operations of a single bank produced, in fifty years, profits equal to $86,000,- 000, or 172 times its original capital. If that bank continues to do business and is allowed to pile up profits in that geometrical progression, it alone, in less than 100 years, will extort from the people all of their property, and—that bank is but one of the 30,000 banks operating on an uneconomic system.

The total capitalization (which includes surplus and undivided profits) of 30,000 banks in 1913, was considerable over $4,000,000,000 and dividends compounded on that sum, as is the custom of banks, will, if allowed to do so by the indifference of the people to their own rights, consume the balance of the nation's wealth.

The accumulated holdings of all the trusts that centralize wealth would immensely reduce the time it will take for the interest and dividends on these holdings to absorb all of our present property, and all of what we earn in the future, except what is required to be left to enable us to eke out a bare subsistence.

But, notwithstanding the community of interest existing between the trusts in order that they may uphold the system that enables them to PAY the LEAST price for wages, farm and other products, and to sell their own services and resell the products controlled by them at the HIGHEST available price, they compete with each other in their efforts to secure the most of our earnings. So, you see, there is competition even between the trusts, and this competition is resulting in their absorption of each other. Anyone with a little imagination and reasoning power can look ahead and see what would be the outcome of that competition if the interests are allowed to carry it to its finish. It is utterly impossible for us to become independent as a nation as long as we are subservient to the present system of excessive interest, dividend, and rent charges,—toll on dead capital. I call attention to the power of a single dollar, and then I ask you to multiply the power of the ONE DOLLAR by the billions that are controlled by a few hundred financial wizards. Here is the table for a single dollar:

The following table, compiled by the Librarian of Congress, illustrates the power of money to enrich the owner through interest accumulations:

One dollar loaned for 100 years at compound interest at

3% per annum would amount to.. $	19.25
6% " " " " " ..	340.00
8% " " " " " ..	2,203.00
10% " " " " " ..	13,808.00
12% " " " " " ..	84,075.00
18% " " " " " ..	15,145,007.00
24% " " " " " ..	2,551,798,404.00

We must bear in mind that there is no difference in principle and final result between interest, dividends, and rents, when the latter are compounded on the capital basis.

It is easily apprehended that the banking institutions alone, by the geometrical progression of accumulation of interest, dividends, and profits, would if left free to do so, take the most of our earnings and property holdings and ut-

terly exhaust our means. We will also find that
the time that will be required to complete this
legalized plunder is still further reduced when
we take into consideration the fact that the
principal stockholders make more profits outside of the banks than they obtain from dividends paid directly to them by the banks.

But it is not necessary for us to wait for the
banks alone to absorb our property and collect
the greater part of our daily earnings, because
there are other great aggregations of centralized capital. The railways alone are valued at
more than a dozen billions of dollars, and by a
decree of the court (not yet overruled, April,
1913) it has been decided that 7% is a reasonable profit for them, and you will find that if
this 7% were to be compounded for a generation and a half it would consume all of the property in existence exclusive of its own, and even
if the rate were to be reduced to 6%, or even
5%, it would only postpone the day of reckon-
ing. Thus, you see, we have another claimant
for our earnings besides the banks—namely,
the railroads.

But even these two are not all. We have the
Standard Oil Company and its subsidiaries,

the Supreme Court decision notwithstanding. There is also the Steel Company and its subsidiaries, the Tobacco Company, the Sugar Company, and various other companies and their affiliations, each of which possesses vast capital so centralized that each separate trust, by the geometrical progression in accumulated interest, dividends, and profits, will require only time in which to consume our present property, as well as our accruing earnings, and, if we allow it, force upon us a state of bankruptcy, because the geometrical progression is impossible to be carried out without so doing. Regardless of this fact, we still have the absurdity of our courts holding that a certain percentage should be a reasonable profit and anything less unfair. If this law were enforced it would ultimately create abject slaves and bankrupts of our children, and we, the parents, should be made to work toward that end. What do you think of that for a democratic government such as ours is supposed to be? Are you going to rest content and permit the political bosses to continue running our government for us? They have had all the past—plenty of time, I am sure

—to remedy such evils. But the story is not yet one-tenth told.

The several trusts cannot, of course, absorb all, but after legally (and otherwise) seizing the principal part of our earnings, they swallow up the smaller of their own kind. The big fishes eat the little ones. As a result, the trusts become less and less in number, but their holdings become greater and greater, the same as the number and holdings of the English landowners. The Government has given its support to the banks by delegating to them the power to issue a substitute for money, and besides that advantage they are depositories for the cash of the people, with which they command a large credit. As a consequence, they have had the inside track in this unequal commercial struggle and they are now largely the masters of business, with the results which I have described.

That is why all of the great trust builders have themselves become bankers. They bought up the larger banks, and control, by a community of interest, most of the smaller ones, as well as influence them all. As late as 1912 James J. Hill absorbed great banking interests in the cities of St. Paul and Minneapolis. He testified before the Money Trust investigating committee that he is a director in three of the greatest banks in New York City, Chicago and St. Paul. I consider Mr. Hill a great, as well as a good man, from the viewpoint of the social order of things that has existed during most of the time in which he has been doing his great constructive work.

We cannot criticize him for the work that he has done, but we should feel that we ourselves are to blame for having allowed the continuance of that system under which he and a few of his associates have been permitted to accumulate so great a part of the result of our earnings. If we had had a proper system, Mr. Hill would have fitted into that as a great constructor. He would have worked with the tools at hand. All great men do. There are other wealthy men of whom we could say the same as we do of Mr. Hill. It is the system to which we should give our first attention and not the men.

The part of the press controlled by the trusts tells us that the corporate stocks are owned by the people—widows, orphans, etc.—and that he who attacks the present system is an enemy to these. It is wonderful how the trusts can find excuses for everything that they do and endeavor to support their system by such sophistry. They stated through the press that the stockholders in these interests number many thousands, and it would seem that they intended to convey to us thereby the idea that we, the people, possess the stock. Some families own stocks in, possibly, as many as a thousand companies. Some individuals own stocks in hundreds, and all of these persons are counted in the total number of stockholders as many times as they own stock in different companies. How many of us own corporate stock of any kind? There are approximately 94,000,000 people in the United States, and there are but a few thousand stockholders with holdings large enough so that the dividends they secure are not assessed back to them in the increased cost of living as a result of this infernal geometrical progression of excessive interest, dividends, and profits, most of which ultimately goes to the big fellows. It is not distributed back to the people, as they attempt to make us believe. Only a small part of it is.

Ex-President Taft suggested to us, through

the medium of a speech, that these things would adjust themselves by the deaths of the holders, and the distribution of the property to their heirs and legatees. He could not have given serious thought to that statement, because we can easily understand that once these things have grown up out of certain conditions they will not disappear as long as those same conditions exist. Besides, even if things were to correct themselves in some unnameable future generation, that fact is not sufficient for the present generation. We have a right to the advantages which God has created for the use of all mankind—and right now. What fools we have been for permitting a few money wizards to use our dire necessities, and our desires for the conveniences and reasonable luxuries of life as a basis for capitalization,—capital on which we must pay interest and dividends to them without any degree of proportion to the true value of the services they render. If we continue to be a government by party—influenced by boss politics and political factions—and allow them to make the laws as we have been doing in the past, we shall be slow in overcoming this one-sided affair.

In a speech made by Vice-President Marshall, in April, 1913, at a New York meeting, is to be found the following statement:

"Suppose a Governor and a General Assembly in the State of New York should repeal the statute of descents for real and personal property and the statute with reference to the making of will on their death, how much vested interest would any relative have in the property which fell from their nerveless hands at the hour of dissolution? The right to inherit and the right to devise are neither inherent nor constitutional, but on the contrary, they are simply privileges given by the state to its citizens."

The Vice-President is absolutely correct. But even if the laws of inheritance were abolished, it would not affect the system by which great fortunes are accumulated. Carnegie, the Rockefellers, the late Jay Gould, E. H. Harriman and J. P. Morgan, and the most of those who have individually amassed wealth by the hundreds of millions, began with little or nothing in the way of capital, except their ability, and the system which permitted their enormous accumulations. As I have already said, it is the system that deprives the plain people of the profits resulting from their work, and gives it to the class of men mentioned. It ought to be of comparatively little satisfaction to this generation to let the system remain unaltered and calmly sit back and allow these enormous fortunes to be accumulated. It is undoubtedly true that the present possessors, if the laws of devise and inheritance were abolished, would dispose of most of it as they wished while still living, but there would be a new set on hand to rob our children. I do not, however, understand that Vice-President Marshall suggested the possibility of abolishing the inheritance laws as a remedy for the social evils complained of.

There is one class of property, however, that I have not mentioned thus far. This is the farm interests. These are the greatest of any single property interest, but these holdings are at the present time diffused among millions of holders, but a geometrical progression of interest, dividends, and profits, in favor of the farmers has never been decreed by the courts. They are not permitted to add interest as a part of the price for which they sell the products of their farms. They must take their chances with the sun, rains and storms, and no court decree has given to them "profits commensurate with the risks" as it has to the railroads and other trusts. The farmer, like the wage earner, lives but to be fleeced by the beneficiaries of the present system. The two, the farmer and the wage earner, support the whole burden of a system which leads continually to immense wealth for the few and bankruptcy or poverty for the rest of us. Farm property has been subject to the highest rates of interest, while all the great industrial properties have been used as a basis for comparatively low rates of interest when money has been loaned on them.

Therefore I repeat my earlier statement, that the only excuse for government is the facility it affords its citizens for securing advantages that operate for the common welfare, which could not be secured with the same degree of equability through independent individual action.

Instead of that our government, which is of our own creation, has insured to the banks and other trusts a system which renders it easy for them to oppress the masses. It enables the few to live as non-producers and exorbitant spenders, while almost the entire burden falls on the rest of us. Such a condition is impossible of long tolerance by the proud, honest and intelligent citizens of our country. We must seek for a remedy.

SHORT SELLING.

We hear many objections raised against short selling, going short in the sales of stocks, securities, grain, provisions, etc., on the market. Short selling means the selling of what the vendor does not possess. In Congress there is pending at all times one or more bills purposed to prohibit this practice. There is, at the present time, serious consideration of passing a bill which will prohibit all short selling, because it is claimed that the practice enables speculators to manipulate the market in a manner that makes it possible for them to pay the producers less and charge the consumers more. This short selling is a much more comprehensive affair than the sponsors of the bills referred to have allowed the public to gather from any expression of theirs which has been given to the public.

It is from the practice of short selling that the bankers derive the greatest profits. That statement will, when first read, meet with resentment and denial on the part of the bankers. It will also surprise many others, but the banker, as well as the others, will admit of its truth when they have fully considered it. If a person were to sell a thousand bushels of wheat or ten shares of stock that he does not own, it becomes necessary for him to go into the market and buy it at the time that he is required to deliver it to the purchaser. Ordinarily, the purchaser on the stock or produce market does not require the vendor to do that, but settles with him for whatever the actual market price is at the time for final settlement. The banker is doing the same thing with the dollar.

All of the money in all of the banks and trust companies combined is only slightly in excess of a billion and a half of dollars, and the banks owe approximately twenty billion dollars. There is not enough money in all of their vaults to pay one-tenth of what they owe. There is not money enough in the whole country, including that outside of the banks, to pay one-sixth of what they owe. That statement may sound a little different from the statement made about the grain and stock gambler, but to those who understand the effect of existing facts,—conditions,—it is clear that the banks are sold short just as effectively as the stock and grain gambler.

Let us follow these facts further as to their reality. No bank could pay its obligations without collecting its outstanding credits. If a simultaneous demand were to be made by all of the creditors of all of the banks, all of the banks would fail. That is because they are all short sold. There is, however, one difference between the banker's practice of short selling, and that of the ordinary stock gambler. The man who borrows from a bank will give his note to the bank, and ordinarily the banker simply credits him on the books of the bank, with the amount of the note less the interest. The bank does not part with the cash, but lets the borrower draw checks upon the account, and, therefore, merely transfers the credit to someone else, for these checks are, in most cases, deposited instead of cashed. The bank continues to draw interest on the note. The party who borrowed sold short to the bank by agreeing to deliver to the bank, when due, the number of dollars that his note calls for, and the bank sold short to the borrower by agreeing to deliver to him that many dollars before the note comes due. Now, in that transaction there were two short sales. The man who borrowed the money agreed to pay at a future date what he did not have when he borrowed, and the banker agreed to pay immediately what he would not have had if he had first paid his other demand obligations. Now, the difference in the way that deal was conducted, and the manner in which the stock gambler carries on his short sales is, that the stock gambler, when a person sells short to him (that is, agrees to sell him stock or provisions to be delivered), does not pay interest to the person so selling. Anyone who carefully investigates the effect of this fact upon the cost of living will find that the short-selling operations of the stock gamblers influence the cost of living far less than the short selling which I have described as being practised by the banks. The banks should not be condemned for this, however, because it is the only way in which the business of the country can be carried on under the present system, or until a new system has been inaugurated.

Every student who has carefully considered this subject knows that the people, as a whole, which includes themselves as individuals, *the General Government, the states and munici-*

palities, cannot pay interest on all of the money
that they have agreed to pay. That is because
money does not create itself. It is claimed that
everyone who has a dollar and loans it out is
entitled to interest. It takes one dollar to furnish the exact equivalent of another dollar. It
takes a dollar to pay a dollar debt, and, since
that is true, there are no dollars left with which
to pay interest. The whole country has sold
money short and could not possibly deliver or
pay the money that it has agreed to pay. The
present outstanding interest-bearing contracts
are rapidly approaching the hundred-billion-
dollar mark. The annual interest alone, con-
tracted to be paid on these obligations, probably
exceeds all of the money in existence. Of
course, some of this interest is paid from other
interest collected and is offset, and the total net
interest is reduced somewhat by that fact, but
the greater part of it still remains to be made
up from other sources.

The only way that interest can be liquidated,
considering the statement in its general application, is by a transfer of the property or the
services of the debtor class to the creditor class.
But, all interest cannot be paid in full even in

that way, because, as we have already seen in a former chapter, the geometrical progression of computing interest accumulates it so rapidly that it would exhaust all there is and fail because of the impossibility of its going further. We, as a people, are in that economic state and cannot extricate ourselves from it under existing conditions. The whole country is sold short by the debtors who have agreed to pay what they have not, and what they cannot get. The creditors "have a corner" on us. How are they enforcing settlement? It is being done in several ways. We are compelled to work more hours per day, receive less pay per hour, pay more for what we buy, and receive less for what we sell. The consequence is that we must work harder and more hours per day than we should, and in the end have less than what is due to us as our part of the advantages, conveniences and opportunities resulting from the advancing civilization. This means absolute destitution for great numbers of the debtor class and an enormous general loss. When I say the debtor class, I do not mean only those who have borrowed money or who owe open accounts. Debt is now one of the most positive influences in our system. The consumer is a debtor because he owes it to the producer to pay his part of the interest and taxes that are added to the cost of production under the present system. As a consequence, we are all virtually debtors, and comparatively few of us have credits and profits enough to offset the debt, or any other way by which to pay it except from the products resulting from our daily toil. Such a condition reduces the general efficiency of the people, and they are compelled to live on a lower scale than they should.

THE POLITICAL ASPECT OF THE PROBLEM OF FINANCES.

When one thinks seriously, and honestly follows the study of the truths previously stated in regard to finances, he realizes that the systems of short selling and others practised by the speculators, who give almost nothing and receive everything in return for their juggling of credits, are of extreme importance when compared with the tariff and the many other problems that are given first consideration by Congress. The statement that the tariff problem should receive the first consideration of Congress is absurd, and has grown out of the trickery of party bosses, and been incorporated into party pretenses as a means of inducing the people to transfer what is called "the responsibility of government" from one party to another, even after both have shown utter incompetence to deal with great problems. The transfer has been made more than once on the tariff issue. It may be interesting to note how many statesmen there are who believe that the cost of living can be reduced by making the people of other countries help to feed and clothe us. It may not occur to them that if a combination can be put up in a country as extensive as the territory of our own, the same methods will ultimately, in fact, already have been extended in a large measure to all of the world. It does not seem to have occurred to them that the tariff is merely an administrative measure and that what might be a suitable tariff measure today may be unsuited to our condition in less than a year. In fact, we shall see in a later study that the whole tariff system as now practiced is false. It is one of the jokers which are used to fool the people from time to time. But, even though we have been fooled into shifting the so-called "responsibility of government" from the shoulders of one party to those of another, when we should have taken it from all parties and placed it where it belongs, with the people, we may, notwithstanding, force the party falsely claiming the sole responsibility for the present government, to aid us in securing reforms in financial legislation that will actually make the people independent of the infernal system now in practice.

The currency and banking problem should

not be a political one in the sense that politics
are commonly understood and considered.
Politics ought to be made a matter of business.
It ought to be taken out of the control of political charlatans and administered by representatives with common-sense business judgments. If
that were done the currency and banking problem, as well as other social problems, would be
dealt with from the standpoint of business principles. Partisanship has been the cause of
retarding all social progress.

The interests have done everything that has
been possible for them to do in order to divide
the people of this country into factions commonly known as political parties, because it was
directly in their interest to do so. The interests
can deal with the political bosses much more
satisfactorily than they could with half or more
of the people's representatives. Party government is factional government and not national
government. Anyone who claims that political
parties are required in order that some one
shall be made responsible for government is
either ignorant or dishonest. Anyone who
claims that all of the people's representatives
cannot rule in the interests of a majority of

their number, better than a political party can rule by a majority of its number, is not informed in the elementary principles of democracy. If there are too many members of a legislative body to make it practicable, reduce their number sufficiently to render it prac-. ticable.

It would seem that the people are too well advanced in their understanding to permit government by caucus, yet that kind of government is practiced by Congress. It is not strange, though, that this false practice is allowed, in view of the fact that the people have not taken a sufficient part in the government, even though the government is entirely their business and they are to blame for the frauds perpetrated upon them. If they paid attention to their own interests the political parties would not be able to run a legislative body that is supposed to represent all of the people and actually represents merely a faction of them.

The one prominent thing that the political parties have done from time to time has been to create jobs for professional politicians. The survival of party government, instead of the administration of the government by the people

for themselves, is due to the people's neglect of
their own best interests. It is not strange, in
view of that fact that the officers, politicians and
job-seekers seek to enrich themselves at the
expense of the people, and run the government
for selfish purposes. The great special interests
have encouraged, both by direct and indirect
means, the division of legislative bodies up into
factions each of which supports some certain
political party. They have furnished aid to the
leading politicians in every possible manner.
But, after all, what are we to do about it?

There is no general rule by which we can distinguish a professional politician from one who
is not. The leaders in the game of politics are
cunning and intellectual, as well as technical
and adroit in their moves, and this adroit cun-
ningness usually increases in proportion to the
increasing information obtained by the people
behind them. There is no sure rule by which
to know who is or is not friendly to the people's government. It requires eternal vigi-
lance, and even that sometimes does not make
timely discoveries. To be observing and keep
informed on general principles is about all that
one can do.

There are some things, however, that may be of aid to a voter. He should be able to discriminate between a reasonable and unreasonable statement made by persons or contained in the press. Take, for instance, the following notice which appeared and was substantially the same in the press generally:

"Mr. Underwood, Chairman of the Ways and Means Committee, and President Wilson will have a conference this evening on the new tariff bill, to determine if it is satisfactory to the Administration."

The next day the press gave notices of the meeting and stated that the bill had been gone over. The purpose of this news item was to impress upon the public mind the idea that the President was directing the legislation. In this connection it is only necessary to suggest to the intelligent that all that the President could possibly learn about the tariff bill in one or two hour conferences, even if several times repeated, might be compared to the impression that a farmer and his team would make on a thousand-acre field after one or two hours of plowing. In fact, all of the statements made about the "directing power exerted by the President over Congress" are folderoy when considered from the standpoint of a proper government. The President has less time to give to the study of any particular bill than any Member of Congress. He is probably the hardest worked man in all of the country, and it is certain that he has less time to give to the study of detailed matters, because of his more numerous duties, than Members of Congress. The President's executive duties alone place upon him a greater burden than that placed upon any other official. He requires a large Cabinet to aid him in carrying out his duties. How could he successfully span his powers over Congress and control the details of even the material provisions of the most important and complicated bills? It is a physical impossibility, and we should not be led to believe that the President can do anything of the kind. Every Member of Congress should feel it his duty to take a vital interest in some part of the work to be done in Congress. The President may exercise a great moral influence over Congress in a broad sense, but we shall have to look to Congress to do its own work—the work that it was created to do. To rely upon the President to do the work of Congress is not only unfair to the President, but it would reduce the efficiency of the Government.

Take, for instance, the recent decision of President Wilson to disassociate the Government from extending any influence or connecting in any way with the so-called "Six Power Chinese Loan." I believe that his action in that matter will be pointed to in the future as of far greater importance and consequence than anything that has recently occurred. But whether it shall be publicly recognized to be so or not, I now believe it to be of very great importance. We may never actually realize what troubles we have avoided by refusing to connect the Government with that deal. The important matters continually coming before the President are manifold, and they give him responsibilities that are too great to permit him to divert his energies and exercise more than a broad moral influence over Congress.

The most important of all human affairs is government, and yet governments exercise less science and less system in their administrations than is exercised by the great Trusts and Corporations in the performance of their business. Is it not time that we administer the Govern-

ment of the United States in the general behalf
by supplying a systematic, scientific and true
economic basis? We can do this and operate it
at least equally as well as the Corporations and
Trusts operate their corporate business in
behalf of their own stockholders. If we are to
accomplish what we desire in that direction we
shall have to stop our partisanship in Congress.
After that each of the Departments of Government will be enabled to render to the people the
service that it was contemplated it should
render when it was originally designed.

GOVERNMENT GUARANTEE OF BANK DEPOSITS.

After the 1907 panic there were many people who advocated the guarantee of bank deposits as a remedy for panics. The guarantee of bank deposits would have little, if any, relation to the cost of living and would not affect any of the fundamental relations of the people with each other. My only reason for considering this subject at all in this book is because it may be raised as an issue in the contemplated banking and currency legislation.

"I have grave fears as to the ultimate success of a guarantee of bank deposits. In the first place, unless there should be some provision prohibiting certain kinds of speculation, or unless human nature should change, even the guarantee of bank deposits will not prevent panics, but will simply defer the day by postponing the hour of fear; for by the very nature of things, when a bull market starts the momentum continues until it reaches a point when economically a breakdown is inevitable.

"There is, in so far as the legitimate industrial pursuits of the country are concerned, both a theoretical and a practical possibility of a self-sustained credit system, based upon monetary foundation, but when you inject into that the complications arising out of speculative gambling, the more you reinforce the system of credit and give an unguarded con-

177

fidence in it, the greater the opportunity the gambling speculators have to fleece us by keeping up a bull market.

"I value confidence when based upon solid economic conditions, but I wish to emphasize the necessity for the people to be suspicious enough to carefully scrutinize the Wall Street manipulations.

"Just as long as we leave that Wall Street gambling contingent, with its allied banks, in a position that enables it to throw its influence into the markets, we are going to have our occasional panic troubles. It seems to me that it would be more advisable to check up accounts more often in order to prevent panics.

"It is probable that if the Government had guaranteed all of the deposits on October last (1907), and continued that guarantee, the panic would not have occurred in that month, but it had to come sooner or later, because the rottenness that caused it would not have been eradicated. Speculative parasites had over-subscribed the credit and crowded out legitimate industry by over-bidding it for the use of the money and credits of the country. If our credit had been still more expansive, and if the people in addition to what they had on deposit had deposited a considerable part of the $1,666,000,000 which they held outside of the banks, industry could have thrived a while longer, but the growth of the speculative parasites would eventually have monopolized the credit. Yes, the speculators would have pushed the bull game, and tossed up the prices until such time as even a Government guarantee could not hold back a panic, and when it did come, it would be greater in its severity in proportion to the amount to which the market was over-bulled, and the fact that the Government was responsible for the guaranteed amount might ultimately destroy the credit of the Government.

"We must not forget that our confidence is the

stock in trade and capital of the professional gambling bulls, and that we must not give them too much of it, nor should we forget that distrust is the stock in trade and capital of the professional gambling bears, and that these two sets of speculators are watching the plain people with the keenest eyes. They rob us on both the rising and falling markets. The bulls catch us when prices go up and the bears when they go down. A satisfactory remedy for panics cannot be gained by creating confidence unless we can eliminate the professional speculators. In other words, we need confidence in legitimate enterprise and distrust in predatory speculation. We plain people must not repose too much confidence in the speculator class of people and thereby permit them to work the confidence game on us to our own ruin. The more confidence we have in our present system, the more we shall lose in the end.

"I have another reason for doubting the advisability of the guarantee of bank deposits. Under the present loose system of examining banks, the doors are left open for easy trickery, which makes it possible for sharpers to rob the people. Let me illustrate: Under our present system it is possible for ten men to combine and start a national bank with 50% of the capital required and to immediately borrow, from the deposits that they secure, enough to recoup their 50% capital, and, in addition, enough to fully pay their stock, so as to leave no capital in the bank except their promissory notes, and, what is more, they are free to repeat that operation by starting a hundred banks in as many different towns and not invest an actual dollar. But even that is not all. The loose way in which banks are examined makes it possible for them to put into the banks the notes of irresponsible parties, which notes might eat up the deposits as rapidly as they are received. No one can prevent this condition, except the bank examiners. I have seen an examiner enter a bank in the morning and finish his examination the same day. During that time he had covered a business of several hundred thousands of dollars, without learning the value of the bills receivable. I have seen this happen again and again in various banks. In the cases that I have observed the bankers have been men of integrity and responsibility. Otherwise they could easily have done all that I have described as possible.

"From what I have said it may easily be seen that a few schemers could abuse the privilege the system gives them. In fact, some of them could so arrange it that their representatives could have large deposits evidenced upon the books of the bank in their control and never have deposited any money, but merely covered the deposits by the class of notes before referred to. Those deposits, under a guarantee system, would be protected unless the fraud could be established. That cannot often be proven, regardless of the fact that it exists.

"If there is to be a guarantee of bank deposits, the guarantee of the deposits of any one person in any one bank should be limited. Under no condition would I be in favor of a guarantee of deposits of the hundreds of thousands and millions of dollars that are owned by single individuals.

"But even the guarantee of the smaller deposits would have its dangers, for those with large deposits, if they became frightened, might make a run for the excess and defeat the very objects of the law. Such a law, again, would, from the standpoint of securing deposits, put the careful, conservative, able and honest banker on the same footing with the careless, indifferent or even dishonest banker. Depositors would also be careless under such a system.

"The above are, I believe, sufficient reasons to prove that it is unwise for the Government to guarantee bank deposits. Nevertheless, I might vote for such a system if the people generally demanded it, because my office is one of representation rather than one in which I can act entirely from my own convictions.

"Let us suppose, for instance, that on October last (1907) instead of a lack of confidence in the bankers, the people should have had so much confidence in them that they had deposited in the banks, and with the trust companies, the most of the $1,666,000,000 that was then in general circulation outside of the banks. What would have happened? The banks would have made loans to anyone from whom they thought they had a fair chance of getting it back. You would now (1908) see such a boom and inflation as has never been known in the history of the world. That might have continued for two, three or four years. What do you suppose the gambling contingent would be doing during that time? Everybody knows. Will somebody answer where a guarantee of bank deposits would land us under such conditions when the crash actually did come?

"The people require a system that will make their capital available in order that they may develop the natural physical resources of the country. Everybody desires to encourage enterprise. I have noticed that when there is active enterprise, there is also a tendency to bull the markets, and the mark is constantly being overshot, because the country is honeycombed with speculators possessing the gambling instinct. Setbacks are the economic penalty and there is not the least possibility, even with a guarantee of bank deposits, of averting them under our present plan of finances."

The above statements are quoted from my speech delivered in Congress after the panic of 1907. Since then I have watched more closely than I had before the way that things have been manipulated, and I am more certain now of the correctness of my statements than I was at the time that I made them. A guarantee of bank deposits would only serve to promote a temporary confidence which would be more completely shattered when it was found that that confidence would be seized upon by speculators to further their selfish interests.

MONEY.

In many respects money is the strangest of all human creations. On the one hand it has civilized the world, and on the other has commercialized and in a manner criminalized the people. But that is not because the purpose of money is erroneous. It is because the office of true money has been usurped by false money, which has served as a false god, and the worship of this false god has caused the degradation of the soul of humanity. None of the dramatic stages through which humanity has passed has been as intense and complicated as that through which it is now passing. That is because a false system has been established, and the longer humanity attempts to struggle forward under it the more severe the struggle will become. Men must appeal to their intelligence to secure for them information in order that they may understand the reason for this false condition in which they find themselves.

For what are we striving? It would seem that our object was to create the most complex conditions and secure the least satisfactory results. As proof of that, we have on the one hand strikes of the poor and underpaid wage earners, and on the other the accumulation of billions of dollars of wealth into the hands of the few, and between the two extremes are those who are paying for it all—the working men and women on the farms, in the shops, in the stores and in all the various occupations that serve to supply mankind with the necessaries of life. Those who gain enormous fortunes as a result of the complex conditions donated approximately $300,000,000 from their superabundance in the single year of 1912 (world). That does not mean that the gifts were sent back to those from whom the wealth had been extorted, but that this vast sum was merely donated to satisfy the whims of those whose first whim it was to extort it from the people. It was generally reported that the late J. Pierpont Morgan, alone, gave to a single museum $50,000,000 in the form of art treasures. How many of the people from whom that great sum was extorted will ever visit the museum or have an opportunity to see those art treasures? Many of them have already gone prematurely to their graves by reason of the overburdensome system that permits the extortion that leaves such a trail of woe in nearly every community. Is it not time that we should understand by what rule a few hundred individuals have inaugurated and been privileged to keep in operation a system which forces the great majority of men to work for them? Surely, our pride as well as our self-interest and sympathy with mankind, generally, ought to force us into more dignified and properly compensated operations.

The secret of the ease with which the millionaires force men generally to work overtime for them, while they accumulate the products of their energy, lies hidden from the most of us in the fact that there is a false measure of value— the "rich man's money," which can be used exclusively by them, instead of a supply of producers' and consumers' money, which would facilitate the exchange of the various products and conveniences of life which could be used for the benefit of all men.

The governments have delegated to the rich the privilege of making the money and charging the rest of us for its use. And the greatest burden of our entire social system is that placed upon us because men are privileged to speculate and gamble in our false money. Neither gold, silver, nor paper are worth anything as money if we take from them the support of the government. Why should we lend our governmental power in order that either gold or paper shall be dignified with a government fiat without consideration? Why should we make it legal tender, and enable the special privileged persons to whom it is given to use the special government stamped gold, or engraved and printed paper as a means of making us pay for the extra value the Government adds by its guarantee? It is even worse than that, for when acting in our governmental capacity if we wish to borrow the government stamped gold and the government fiat paper from those to whom the stamp was given, we are forced to pay usury. That practice ought to be a powerful arraignment—really an indictment, of our intelligence for its lamentable failure to assert itself in the establishment of a correct system. Have we the intelligence and perseverance to prosecute the indictment until the conviction is complete? If we have, the conviction will free all mankind from its present state of bondage, because, contrary to the practice in criminal jurisprudence of paying the penalty or serving the sentence after the conviction, in this case we have already paid the penalty.

What is it that makes money of a piece of gold, or of a slip of engraved and printed paper? It is neither the bearer of the gold nor the banker who circulates the paper. It is the Government guarantee of the people's credit and support that gives it currency. Not a cent of the value that is in the gold coin, excepting its worth in the sciences and the arts, rightfully belongs to the owner of the bullion. Not a penny in a bank bill, whether it be a five, ten, or greater number of dollars, rightfully belongs to the banker until he has paid for it the same as the rest of us are obliged to pay in order to get them. Whatever power of purchase there is in either, exclusive of the base metal value in the one and the trivial paper value in the other, is purely of governmental origin—and that is the people's credit.

If we were to take from the gold coin the governmental legal tender stamp, it might not be worth 10 per cent of its present value, and if we were to do the same with the bank bills they would not sell for a cent a pound. But we who

by the sweat of our toil support these, have
given them to the special interests to juggle with
and manipulate, thereby creating millionaires
and idlers on the one side, and paupers and
toilers on the other. It is this money that we
support and give to the rich to juggle with that
makes the products of our toil of comparatively
small service to ourselves.

The high cost of living is traceable to the failure of the Government to exercise its functions
"to regulate the value" of money. The Government stamps its fiat on gold and paper, but
the stamping process favors the interests alone
and results in their controlling the people's
products. This fact has so complicated our industrial and commercial relations that we have
financial gamblers, speculators, and unbearable
complications as a result. It seems to have
reversed the very purpose for which we live,
and in the greedy struggle for individual wealth
civilization trembles in the balance. All men
compete for the possession of the money that by
a single act could be demonetized, a true
money created, and the world delivered from its
bondage to Mammon.

It seems almost superfluous to refer to the

fact that money should be of stable measure in purchasing those things which are required to supply the daily requirements of men, but that is not the kind of money we now have. As we have already observed, we use the rich men's money and pay them so great a usury that most of our time is occupied in toiling to earn it. The rich men's money is scarce or plentiful, according to the manner in which they use it, and their dollars vary from time to time in their purchasing power, which renders them an unstable standard, one on which men cannot depend.

Is there any more reason why the men who get the gold and those who secure bank charters should be able to come to us, and demand that we the people—the Government—should coin the gold and engrave and print the paper and impress on these a fiat and legal tender character, while they manipulate and gamble in our products, than there is that we should use wheat, corn, cotton or any other product of our labor or land, or even applied labor itself, as a basis on which to establish credit, and we the Government fix a measure of legal tender based upon these commodities and the properly applied energy of men as a security? If we are going to continue that practice, we should be impartial and establish it for the benefit of all men and not for a favored few. Unfortunately, we have been educated to extend personal and special property favoritism which has resulted in the formation of an aristocracy by those so favored. They have segregated themselves and appropriated most of the advantages that have resulted from new inventions and better methods of application. They appropriate most of the enjoyments of life, while the rest of us are forced to toil and struggle in order to support the system that makes the present social and industrial conditions possible. The people have secured comparatively few of the advantages of the system that has permitted the few to be immeasurably extravagant and inconsiderate of the general welfare.

Let me instance the following as an apt and timely illustration of the above.

"H. T. HATFIELD,
"Shoreham Hotel.
"April 22nd, 1902.
"To Hon. CHARLES A. LINDBERGH,
"House of Representatives.
"DEAR SIR:—
"On Thursday of this week the Woolworth Building in New York City, the highest building in the world, is to be opened with a banquet.

"More than one hundred Members have already signified their acceptance of the invitations to be present at this banquet. For the convenience of the Members of Congress a special train de luxe will be run from Washington to New York, leaving the Union Station at Washington on Thursday, 10:55 A. M., arriving at New York at 3:55 P. M. Limousines will meet this special to convey the party to the Waldorf-Astoria.

"Following the banquet in the evening, another special train will bring Members back to Washington, arriving here at 8 A. M.

"We would very much appreciate your presence at this banquet. A ticket of identification, providing for a round-trip passage on the special train, and all incidentals, is being mailed you from New York. These tickets are not transferable, however. The courtesy will be appreciated if you will notify Mr. H. T. Hatfield, care of Shoreham Hotel, Washington, D. C., of your acceptance.

"Kindly do your utmost to be with us on this happy occasion.

"Very sincerely yours,
"H. T. HATFIELD."

I do not cite the above as an exception, for things of that character are the common practice. It is probable that in this case there are no axes to be ground. It may have been a mere courtesy to invite the Members. But we do know that things of this kind are going on all of the time and they have a tendency to make people believe them to be right, whereas they are absolutely wrong. The invitation, if generally accepted, would involve a cost of many thousands of dollars for the entertainment of the Congressmen alone. The total cost of such an entertainment would be charged to the cost of the building and added to the rents paid by the tenants, and the tenants will charge it back to those whom they serve, and finally it will come back to be paid by the people. Considered from a broad viewpoint, there is only one proper way to act in all of these matters in order that they should be fair, and that is to have every person pay for what he gets and get pay for what he does for others. If that were done we should have no paupers and no poor in the degree that we now have. It is this special favoritism that is being so extensively practiced in all sorts of ways that is doing so much mischief. President Wilson set a good example when he announced that he would not accept any gratuitous offerings from theatres, clubs or other source. To those who are unfortunate and in need we ought to give, but those who are able to work ought to be properly paid for what they do, and afterward pay for what they get.

I have been waiting patiently for several years for the opportunity to expose the false money standard and to show that the greatest of all favoritisms is that extended by the Government to the Money Trust. I realized that no person possessed within himself the power to bring this stupendous problem before all of the people—and further, that the psychological time would have to come in order that the people should take an interest and study and understand it sufficiently to reinforce the efforts of any person undertaking to present the real truth (and practically the whole of it) concerning the present system, and that that time would probably be when the Money Trust and special interests were seeking to further gouge the people. I knew further that eventually these greedy soulless creatures would attack their own standard—the GOLD DOLLAR— because great as has been its aid in helping them to enslave humanity and absorb the results of the people's energy, it could not satisfy their increasing greed. That greediness knows no limit, and they are now attacking their own system because it does not give them as much power as they desire. Under its present form they control the finances and consequently the industries. But, they now wish for still more. They would further defraud the people, and while they seek to prove that the gold standard is false, they still seek to retain it as a measure, by advocating a new standardization of it. Their own struggle to prove the falsity of the gold standard, after all of the years they have spent in teaching the people to believe in it as sacred and inviolable, has brought about the psychological time for the people to impress upon themselves the whole truth concerning money and the present financial system. You will find my conclusions on the subject in the next chapter.

THE REMEDY.

All that one needs to do in order to be convinced of the need for reforms is to observe men in their different social conditions. Study them in their homes, on their farms, in their shops and places of business. It is in the homes that we find the results of our industrial relations. All places of industry are simply quarters where work is done and business transacted in order to supply the necessaries of life that are required principally in the homes. Enter the palaces of the capitalists and you will find them filled with luxuries. The owners revel in extravagance and waste. Servants answer every beck and call and do for them the things that healthy people ought to do for themselves. The world responds to the demands of the rich. In the home of the average farmer you will find its occupants employing frugality, temperance and self-support. They have little luxury and no excesses. The farmer is the mainstay and the balance wheel of humanity, yet the world makes no recognition of him except to demand the food that he is instrumental in producing. Go into the home of the wage earner. In most cases he is a tenant. You will find that, on the average, he lacks many of the necessaries of life. His product is labor, and it is in demand everywhere, but the world makes no recognition of him except to insist that he sell his labor as cheaply as they demand. He is forced to live beneath the value of his service. These statements do not cover all that we should know, but they are suggestions as to where anyone may obtain full information on the results of our present social order.

If one is satisfied to know that such a difference exists between the conditions of people in the different stations of life as a comparison of each class will show to exist, then he need not be interested further in this discussion. But those who have a sympathy with and a desire for a betterment of existing conditions will be prepared to compare the cost of the remedies proposed with the advantages that would result.

We cannot disregard the established order of civilization. It is the result of the growth of centuries and all of our institutions are moulded around it. The present generation possesses

new ideas, but we have old institutions and we
know that we cannot put our new ideas into
execution without discarding some of the old
institutions. Those who have secured special
privileges and are snugly fitted into the old
conditions which are a result of old methods
will strenuously resist new innovations. A
transition from the old to the new will necessarily create some disturbance because of that
opposition. Moving from an old-fashioned
house into a new one which has all of the
modern improvements involves the inconven-
ience of readjustment, but it is the added convenience that they know will come after the
adjustment that induces people to make
the change. Likewise in changes involving
economic problems we will at first have some
inconveniences. Changes are not justified
unless it is evident that an improvement of conditions will be the result.

We have previously observed that the defects
of our financial system are fundamental. It
breaks down by its own weight. Interest com-
puted on the use of centralized capital and
enforced on the present basis creates inequality
as a matter of course. This is an absolute fact.

We shall have some inequality under any
system because we are not born equal except in
theory, but, the very fact that we are not born
with equal physical power and brain force, nor
into equally favorable environments, and that it
is impossible to bring about conditions that
would accomplish such equality even within a
long period of time, should cause us to seek
more earnestly to make the political and social
conditions such that the less skillful and the
less favorably situated, whether it be in financial affairs or otherwise, will not be robbed of
the results of whatever manner of service they
are best fitted by nature to perform. The
artificial difference which results from legal and
social discrimination it is within our power,
and therefore our duty, to overcome. We cannot expect perfection under any state, but a
vast improvement in the conditions of all men
can easily be brought about.

In seeking success in life, the main require-
ment is to have the necessary instruments for
a practical application of our time and energy,
so that we may secure the things that are necessary and desirable for us to have in order that
we may live in a state of usefulness and indi-

vidual effectiveness as well as of happiness. That means that in some form òr other we should continue in useful activity, that we should fit into some natural station in the social order of things, and because under a state of civilization such as ours is, many things are necessary to each of us, we must rely on each other to supply what we do not individually produce or control. That means a great interchange of service, material and all manner of commodities. There must be a means of measuring values so that this exchange may be made on as nearly an equable basis as is possible. In other words, we require some measure of value. Most of us immediately associate that idea with money.

The kind of money we have been using has failed to promote justice in our daily relations. We have had to resort most often to credit because money alone failed and the interest charge on both money and credit has been too great for us to pay. Still, we must use the present system until we can provide another, because if we do not have some means of exchange there will be stagnation and consequent deterioration. Industry is necessary, and when one produces more useful things than he can use it is desirable that they be transferred to someone needing them. But the vendee may at that time have no articles that the vender may be in need of, and while the vender may not be in any need of the goods or services of the purchaser at the time of the sale, it is still necessary for him to secure for his benefit a credit that he may convert at some future time into that which will supply his demands at the time of such conversion. It is the function of money to supply that credit. That is the only capacity that money should possess. Honest money is nothing but credit.

Creating money out of commodities like gold and silver and legislating value into them by making them legal tender is the worst possible policy and the greatest limitation placed upon advancing civilization. It is the same in principle, though not in degree, as would be the printing and giving of legal tender paper money by the Government to persons who give no consideration in return. No especial value should be legislated into property. Neither gold nor any other metal or commodity should be stamped with a value and made a legal tender.

Commodities may properly be stamped with their quality and weight so that the stamp may be accepted as the proof thereof. After that they may be used as exchange in commerce on their own commercial merits. Neither person nor property is entitled to any specially conferred governmental privileges. To coin metal and make it a legal tender gives a special value to the metal which enables those possessing it to take undue advantage of the rest of us. But I do not advocate the immediate repeal of the law covering this condition, because such an act might disconcert business and do much immediate harm. I would, however, have men know the truth and seek a remedy. That will not disconcert business or do harm.

To reverse our financial system and to stop the extortions now practiced would be to make a tremendous change. If it involved only the parasites—those living on speculation and other parasitic devices—we could in good conscience make the change however abruptly it might end their practice. But the present system involves also those who are engaged in legitimate business. It was accepted in good faith and acted upon by them. All commercial transactions are based upon it. Contracts which extend far into the future depend upon it for their very value, and many people's savings have been measured on this basis. These things cannot be overthrown abruptly without bringing about a state of financial and industrial chaos. It will readily be seen that this is a most serious matter, involving on the one hand the protection of those legitimately interested in pending incomplete deals as well as business arrangements based upon the present system, and on the other the rank and file of the people, and also the coming generations. There is equity on both sides, and the problem is to act justly and while making the change to give as little trouble as is possible and yet remain firmly determined to secure a system that will insure stable, lasting and equitable social relations between all of the people.

No one giving this subject intelligent and impartial consideration will claim that mere amendments to the present financial system will cure our economic evils. We may relieve it of some of its administrative defects by making a few simple amendments and use it during the period of transition from the old system to an entirely new system that shall be based on true economics capable of practical application.

The use of a double system during this transition period would give us an opportunity to adjust by natural selection. The extension of the old system, modified to remove some of its administrative defects, will protect our old institutions and their concurrent obligations. The establishment of a true fundamental system of exchange which will gradually displace the old will relieve us of its burdens after such time as will be necessary in order to fulfill existing obligations. We should immediately get the benefit, and all people both of the present and future generations may in that way be justly dealt with.

We have found that the manipulation of credit has been the most potent of all methods employed by financiers as a means of controlling commerce and fixing prices. It has made virtual kings of some men in the field of finance, and through its power they support a system that gives to the actual producers the least return and to the consumers the greatest expense possible, considering that they must leave enough for the people to work out a bare sub-

sistence. We are all consumers and should all
be producers, and, therefore, are all interested
in the results to be obtained from our activity
in whatever form we apply it.

No individual or private concern should be
allowed to control credit, except that credit
based upon actual production or a service, the
results of which practically correspond in value.
To allow individuals to create conditions or take
advantage of the existing conditions in such a
way that they are enabled to secure a credit
that is not based upon actual production equal
in value to the credit, is as plainly a tax upon
humanity as if government bonds were issued
and the people were obliged to pay them.

Take for example the watered stock issued,
and the fee received, by J. P. Morgan & Co., for
organizing the U. S. Steel Co. J. P. Morgan &
Co.'s fee was $62,500,000 and at least $500,-
000,000 of watered stock was issued. Utimately
that stock gets into the hands of so-called "innocent purchasers," that is, those stockholders
who were not parties to the original graft.
While the fees of J. P. Morgan & Co. were in
the form of bonds or stocks in the hands of
the company and the other incorporators held

the rest of the watered stock, at least $500,-
000,000 of that stock was graft. But, when
J. P. Morgan & Co. and the others sell their
watered stocks and bonds, then the buyers are
the so-called "innocent purchasers," and so, by
some closely drawn and refined distinction of
financialdom, suavely communicated to the
business world, and practically fostered by the
courts, it is called an obligation upon the public,
the implication being that the public, which includes the children of this and future generations, are negligent or guilty. They pay the
dividends and watered stock by having them
added to the price of the necessaries of life.
Of course any one giving this subject proper
consideration knows that such a construction is
based upon the subserviency to a false system;
that is, a misconception of the fitness of the
rule. That policy will have to be overruled
and the court finally adopt a construction which
will not destroy the right of the public to sur-
vive.

In the meantime J. P. Morgan & Co. and the
others will invest the receipts from the sale of
their watered stocks and securities in the securities of railways or other industries in which

there is also likely to be more or less water. But, in both cases, after these sales and purchases take place, we have what are called "innocent purchasers." As between the so-called "innocent purchasers" and the general public the decree of the court is that the public shall pay the penalty by having it added to the freight bills, passenger fares and other necessaries required. One point removed, the original graft seems to be merged into an actual investment— so-called bona-fide. In this case the investor who buys to speculate on the public demand, and who had the privilege of investigating before he purchased, is by the rules of procedure placed in a more secure position than the public which could not investigate. We cannot expect anything approaching social justice as long as we tolerate such a condition as this, or any system which enables private concerns, individual or otherwise, to appropriate credit that is not based upon a service or production that corresponds in value to the credit created. All honest credit is the result of social conditions and belongs to the public, and should be used by the public for the common welfare.

It is clearly evident that if we are to correct

the social evils we must first have an honest
means of exchange. When we have an honest
means of exchange the complications of government will be almost infinitely simplified. When
the individual citizen knows that his service to
other citizens is generally compensated in proportion to its value, the whole social fabric will
be inspired with confidence, and individual
initiative will everywhere be manifested and
general prosperity permeate all departments.
It is because we have allowed individuals to
appropriate the public credit that we are now
in an industrial chaos in so far as doing equity
is concerned. We have the motive powers and
there is sufficient in nature to supply our reasonable requirements, only the means of distribution have been misapplied and the waste
appalling and the majority of us are unable to
supply our reasonable requirements.

We shall have to revert back to fundamental
principles in order to secure a foundation on
which to build intelligently and satisfactorily,
and reach a proper social and financial condition. There is no escape from that course and
we should not seek any, because it is the natural
thing to do, but it is what we have failed to do in
the past.

We are now face to face with problems pertaining to legislation and the making of provisions for administrative measures. If these problems are to be properly solved they must receive the attention and concentration of men whose faculties of judgment are based upon experience in personal and business contact, and proceed from calm minds with no fear. All should join this great undertaking, but all should remain wholly uninfluenced by personal or political prejudice. No right of preference exists in favor of persons, property, or business. The nation as a whole should establish administrative measures which will foster conditions that will prove satisfactory for the greatest period of time. It should, however, give due regard to the fact that the proper exercise of individual initiative and freedom is the greatest inducement to industry and that personal claims and ambitions must yield in favor of whatever best serves the general welfare.

THE GOLD STANDARD.

On March 14, 1900, the Money Trust, after carrying on an adroit campaign covering a con-

siderable period, secured from Congress an act
which called for the permanent establishment
of the so-called "gold basis" for all of our
money. Since then there have been new inventions made for mining gold which make the
available amount more plentiful, with the result
that the "gold basis" is puzzling the Money
Trust. But there is a still further complication
and that is that the people are becoming
familiar with the fallacy of the "gold standard"
and they are becoming dissatisfied in proportion to their understanding of its bad effects.

The dollar is worth less now than it was in
1900, that is, it will buy less. That fact, particularly, does not satisfy the creditor class.
They have had enormous interest returns, but
they have lost a part of that advantage because
of the depreciation of the purchasing power of
the dollar. To a greater or less extent all of
the people are dissatisfied with it; many for
selfish reasons and they only desire a remedy to
be adopted which will help them alone, but there
are fewer of these than there are of those who
seek a reform which will better the conditions
of all. Such a remedy would not satisfy the
Money Trust.

We have seen many comments in the press lately in regard to a plan devised by Professor Irving Fisher of Yale University. Mr. Fisher is no doubt an honest and earnest worker who is trying to reform the gold standard. He has arrived at the inevitable conclusion that every capable student must finally accept, and that is that the present gold standard is not the standard by which we can secure honest money.

Professor Fisher has given a most thorough analysis of the production and supply of gold and shown quite extensively the effect of its present use as a money standard upon the prices of commodities. The Fisher plan is now prominently before the country. The professor is a man of eminent ability and reputed to be thoroughly honest in his purpose. I have given below a synopsis of his plan as stated in the Boston *News Bureau* of Dec. 28, 1912. It is as follows:

* * *

"Professor Fisher is one of the most distinguished economists in this country, if not in the world. He is eminently practical and not merely theoretical in all his work and writing."

* * *

"All who have to do with long-time contracts

recognize the desirability of a monetary unit of
fixed purchasing power."

* * *

"The following is Professor Fisher's plan for converting the gold dollar into such a composite unit,
thus standardizing the dollar. Such standardization
would be effected by increasing or decreasing the
weight of gold bullion constituting the ultimate dollar in such a way that the dollar shall always buy
the same average composite of other things."

* * *

"Every dollar in circulation derives practically its
value or purchasing power from the gold bullion with
which it is intercontrovertible. Every dollar is now
intercontrovertible with 25.8 grains of gold bullion
(nine-tenths fine), and is therefore worth whatever
this amount of bullion is worth."

* * *

"The very principle of intercontrovertibility with
gold bullion which we now employ could be used to
maintain the proposed standardized dollar. The
government would buy and sell gold bullion just as
it does at present but not at an artificially and im-
mutably fixed price."

* * *

"At present the gold miner sells his gold to the
mint receiving $1, in (say) gold certificates, for each
25.8 grains of gold, while, on the other hand, the
jeweler or exporter buys gold of the government,
paying $1 of certificates for every 25.8 grains of
gold. By thus standing ready to either buy or sell
gold on these terms ($1 for 25.8 grains) the govern-
ment maintains exact parity of value between the
dollar and the 25.8 grains of gold. Thus the 25.8
grains of gold bullion is the virtual dollar."

* * *

"The same mechanism could evidently be employed

to keep the dollar equivalent to more or less than 25.8 of gold, as decided upon from time to time."

* * *

"The change in the virtual dollar (bullion weight of gold intercontrovertible with the dollar) would be made periodically or once a month, not by guesswork, or at anybody's discretion, but according to an exact criterion. This exact criterion is found in the now familiar "index number" which tells us whether the general level of prices is, at any time, higher or lower than it was. Thus, if in any month the index number was one per cent above par, the virtual dollar would be increased 1%. Thus the dollar would be 'compensated' for the loss in the purchasing power of each grain of gold by increasing the number of grains which virtually make the dollar."

My manuscript for this book was about completed when I first saw the notice of Professor Fisher's plan and I wrote him for the details of his plan. He sent me full information and among other things the article, a part of which I have quoted above. Professor Fisher has performed a great service to his country and to the world by discrediting the gold standard so convincingly. When a man of his prominence and ability has the courage to state his beliefs, the more timid of those holding like views, of which there are many, ought to take an active part in supporting the indictment of the gold standard.

While the Professor has clearly indicted the gold standard and conclusively shown that it is a false one, I do not agree with the remedy that he proposes. Instead of proposing to abandon gold as a standard, and relegating it to its natural place among the articles of commerce, he advocates its reform and would still retain it as a standard by making the weight of the dollar variable and determining its value from time to time according to a commodities index. The Professor is surely correct in his assumption that commodities have actual value worth considering in connection with the establishment of a true exchange system based upon the actual value of services and commodities. I regret that Professor Fisher has complicated the conclusions he arrives at by continuing to consider the gold standard entitled to any greater recognition than is accredited to commodities in general. After proving its falsity, I believe he should have suggested the abandonment of the gold standard.

If we were compelled to change the weight of the dollar monthly, quarterly, or even annually, as we would have to do with a commodity dollar, if we tried to keep it of the same purchasing power all of the time, it would give us more trouble than we now have in changing the tariff schedules.   But while Professor Fisher has performed a world service in being instrumental in giving general publicity to the falsity of the gold standard, that publicity is pushed by the influence of the selfish interests, because they are pleased with the remedy he proposes.   If he had not proposed to standardize the gold dollar, his proof that it is not an honest measure of value would have received no publicity greater than he himself and his friends and a few others could give to it.   It would have been ridiculed if he had not proposed a remedy that suited the interests, for the money sharks demand some measure that is favorable to them and not fair to the people. They have always sought to make the world believe the gold standard to be sacred and, therefore, that the people were bound to support it no matter how much it wronged them. These selfish interests have simply seized on this proposed remedy, which I believe Professor Fisher to have erroneously suggested without his having given as much thought to the remedy as he had to the facts which conclusively prove gold to be a false money standard.

It may seem strange to some people that this remedy suggested by Professor Fisher should be advertised all over the world now, but there is nothing strange about it, for the all-powerful Money Trust interests are quick to observe anything that might be made use of by them, and immediately upon its appearance they seized upon the idea of standardizing the Gold Dollar and were instrumental in having the plan advertised in order, if possible, to induce the people to accept it as a remedy.

It may not be generally realized by the people that this is a critical period in the establishment of governmental policies, but the interests are especially alert to that fact. Everything is being done to make the people accept some worthless, makeshift, and in some cases actually harmful, so-called "remedies," which, if accepted, will delay the adoption of real substantial remedies until another generation shall enter public life. Simultaneously, in all countries where they have the gold standard (and that is in most countries, and in the others equally unjust standards are used) articles were

published which were substantially the same in
substance as the following which was published
in the *Washington Press,* on April 12th, 1913.

"To Ask International Gold Dollar Agreement.
  "One of the features of the proposed currency legislation which will be considered by Congress is the
initiation of a movement for an international agreement for the purpose of preventing the depreciation
of the gold dollar.
  "Such action has been suggested by eminent
economists. It is widely held that the enormous
increase in gold supply and the consequent depreciation of the gold dollar is the real cause of the high
cost of living and high prices.
  "Democratic leaders, especially Senator Owen,
chairman of banking and currency, feel that if the
cost of living is to be reduced the gold situation must
be taken into account."

Not all of the articles appearing in the press
directly discuss the gold standard, but many
of them are adroitly written in order to impress
the reader and fit him to receive the fact that
the gold dollar is not now a good standard, but
further designed to make the reader come to
a wrong conclusion on the question of a remedy.
When the first half of an argument is true,
unless the reader is very careful it goes far
toward making him believe that the second half
is also true, and that is frequently the case
even when the conclusions are wholly erroneous,

as long as the material is adroitly handled. That is where the danger to the people comes in this discussion of the gold standard. Innumerable articles are now published, in fact the plan is systematically advertised, for that very purpose. But there are other articles which are written and published in good faith and in these there is no intention to deceive. An article was published in *Collier's Weekly,* also on the date of April 12th, 1913, which I quote below, by permission. The article is well written and true, but does not suggest a remedy. It leaves the reader at sea as to what shall be done. Readers may fall into the hands of other writers who will mould their opinions and cause them to draw wrong conclusions unless they possess the time in which to make a thorough study of the problem. Very few actually have sufficient time. No one will deny that it requires a great deal of time and patience to understand the banking and currency problems and its relations to business and speculation.

Following is the article from *Collier's:*

"THE DISCOURAGEMENT OF THRIFT.

"The people of the United States have now saved up well over a hundred billions, as measured by current money standards. The aggregate is amazing, and, while the amount per capita is not large, nothing like it was ever known before in any country. This saving takes on many forms—the largest, of course, being in the rearing of children—which shows itself in the steady increase in the value of land. The next is ownership of enormous amounts of securities, of railway and industrial companies, and the like. Then probably comes life insurance. The savings in banks are relatively small. The increment in land values goes to much less than one-half of the population, even in theory, and a comparatively small number of people get the benefit which is made up of the efforts of all. The larger amount of the securities outstanding represents a more or less fixed value. The eighteen billions of insurance in force is of absolutely fixed value. While these securities and insurance obligations were being created, the relative worth of the dollar has been rapidly declining. The forehanded folk who saved and loaned this money get for it an average return of less than 5 per cent, and if they received back the principal now it would buy, of land or food, one-third less than twelve or fifteen years ago. This is a savage penalizing of thrift. We believe that events will soon focus public attention upon this serious problem. The procedure of the insurance companies, which in part is enforced by law, is of special interest. The companies collect above $600,000,000 annually from policy holders and from this loan largely on long-time notes. They act simply as money brokers; but with this effect, that with the rapid depreciation of the currency in the last fifteen years, they are now returning to their policy holders, on death claims or matured policies, relatively far less than the average amount of money which the policy holders have paid in. Roughly speaking, the policy holder has been paying in one-dollar bills; he will get back sixty-six-cent pieces. Theoretically, the compounding of the interest on premiums ought to pay the companies expenses and yield the policy holders a profit on the average payment. In point of fact, with the extravagance of the companies and the decline in the purchasing power of the dollar, there is a serious loss. This is not as it should be. A remedy might lie in a radical change of investment. A larger part of the insurance money is loaned directly or indirectly on land. Actual ownership of the land ought to be as safe as loans, and, if gold inflation is to continue, more profitable. It is something to think about."

Surely *Collier's* states the truth when it says that it is something to think about. We have indeed been buncoed long enough, so long that we ought to think about it seriously now. But we ought not to be led to postpone a real remedy by giving any credence to this so-called standardization of the gold dollar. If we adopt that idea we shall go on with as many troubles as we have now and with that one added.

A TWO-FOLD REMEDY REQUIRED.

As already indicated, I believe that the remedy is necessarily two-fold:

First, and concurrent with the establishment of a new system, the old system should be so amended that some of its most serious administrative defects will be diminished. It should then serve as a vehicle for carrying out the equitable relations and obligations already existing as a result of the legitimate business based upon it.

Second, an entirely new system should be instituted which shall be founded upon the natural demands of commerce and trade and divorced from personal favor or property preference. This new system should be the basis for the establishment of a permanently solid and equitable means of exchange.

In order to completely accomplish the latter, we will have to cease monetizing gold, silver, or other metal or commodity. But that prohibition would not prevent, nor should we desire to prevent, the use of these metals as a means of exchange. The Government, on being paid the cost of stamping, may properly stamp the weight and quality on any commodity of commerce and let it pass in exchange on a basis of its own intrinsic value. Anyone who demands more than that privilege for the use of a metal or other commodity is intentionally unfair to the rest of us, or ignorant. In most cases it is because the persons accept seeming facts without actually understanding the conditions which surround them. If the owner of gold, silver, or other commodity, whether it be wheat, corn, or other produce capable of being stored and preserved, desires to pay the Government the expense of the operation, there need be no objection to our Government giving a certificate of ownership transferable on delivery. If it is done in one metal or commodity, it should be applied to all commodities practicable to be handled, and the person holding the certificate should be able to secure that commodity upon presenting the certificates of ownership and paying the costs of storing. The transaction would then cancel the certificate. But we have a complete, and I claim an indisputable, right, as sovereign citizens, to deny to holders of gold the present privilege of hav-

ing their gold monetized by government stamp.
To so stamp gold and make it legal tender is
simply to decrease the value of our labor, and
of our property—if we have any, unless we also
possess gold enough to offset, which most of us
do not.

The owners of gold claim that it has an intrinsic value which makes it the most practicable commodity to use as money. Because of
its small bulk it is a convenient commodity to
ship and store. But, it can be used as a means
of exchange without making it legal tender.
The Government could still stamp its weight
and fineness, and then it could be exchanged
in the same way that it now is if it really is
intrinsically worth what they say. If it is not,
then it should be exchanged for only what it is
worth. When the owners of gold ask anything
more, they, in effect, admit that it becomes more
valuable with the legal tender privilege than
without. They would not demand it if that
were not true. It cannot be made legal tender
except by governmental act. A governmental
act is the act of the people and there is no
reason why the people should stamp gold or
any other commodity that belongs to individ-

uals with a special privilege. This results in a tax against themselves. Let gold be weighed and tested and given credit only for what it is. Existing coins will retain their legal tender while in circulation, but when the Government acquires any such their legal tender character will be removed and after that bullion should be stamped with its weight and quality and should become an article of commerce standing on its own merits.

If the owners of gold are correct in their statement that gold circulates on its intrinsic value, instead of partly on that and partly on the additional value it acquires by reason of the demand created by the legal tender stamp, it is useless for them to ask that it be made legal tender, and if gold is not commercially worth what it circulates for as legal tender, then the owners are unjust in asking the public to support the value added to gold by the government stamp. Let them take whichever side of that proposition they wish. In the one case the legal tender quality would be useless. In the other it would be a burden placed upon the public and supported for the benefit of the owners of gold.

To cease monetizing gold or metal is to drop
a practice long indulged in for the benefit of the
money loaners. The people have become accustomed to paying them for the credit supported
by themselves. I cannot say that it can be
entirely stopped. There are many practices
that injure the people generally, but are nevertheless followed. I simply call attention to certain facts that cannot be successfully disputed.
I know, and so does any careful student know,
whether he admits it or not, that the fact that
the Government stamps legal tender privileges
on gold creates an increased and artificial demand for it, and consequently a merchantable
value that is very much in excess of what it
would be if the gold did not have impressed
upon it this legal tender privilege. In my
judgment, the value that gold would possess if
it were demonetized would not exceed ten per
cent of its present cost. It now partakes of the
character of monopoly. Every additional cent
of credit given to it above its intrinsic worth as
an article of commerce, by reason of the Government's stamping it legal tender, is first extorted from the people's own credit, next accumulated in the form of so-called "capital,"

and after that becomes the basis for charging them compound interest for generations—perpetually—if they shall not emancipate themselves by an abandonment of this false practice. As far as the principle is concerned, there is no difference between the Government stamping gold as legal tender and giving the owner the advantage of its increased value, and the same stamping process being applied to plain paper.

Under the present practice all value in excess of what gold is actually worth as an ordinary article of commerce is fiat-credit added to it by the people. If the same stamp were affixed to paper it would all be fiat. It is simply a question of degree, and neither can be extended to the individual as a free privilege without robbing the people of all that is added by their credit.

The whole problem simply reduces itself to a question of how long the people desire to remain industrial slaves to a false system. The gold owners ridicule fiat green backers, yet they themselves are fiatists. If they are not, why do they object to gold circulating on its own commercial merits? Why do they wish to coin it with any other designation than its weight and

fineness, and why force the people to take it as
legal tender? They are inconsistent in claiming
a special privilege for gold. If gold is worth all
they claim for it, it needs no extra function. If,
on the other hand, it is not able to retain its
present relative value without being legal
tender, then that is positive proof that it should
not be made legal tender. In the one case it is
unnecessary, in the other case it is unjust. The
Government will have to cease monetizing gold
or any metal as soon as the people generally
realize its present imposition on them.

You may say that some losses would be suffered in a readjustment. That will of course
be admitted, but the losses would not begin to
equal those that are continually taking place
now. The excessive interest and expense of
maintenance resulting from the use of the false
system under which we operate is so great that,
notwithstanding all of the modern inventions
that have immensely increased the people's productive energy, most of us fail to secure the
ordinary advantages that are due from this
civilization to every honest, industrious person.
The interest, dividend and rent charges alone,
compounded as they are now, are absolutely

sure to keep the greatest number of us in want, and many of us in misery.

I do not say demonetize gold. I simply say cease to monetize it. Coin no more metal with the legal tender character attached, except that required for small change. Our gold will circulate in foreign markets on its weight and quality equally well without the legal tender attachment as long as foreigners will use it for their legal tender. Gold will do that as an article of commerce, and foreign nations may convert it into their own legal tender if they like, but any nation that uses gold as legal tender after a great nation like our own ceases to do so will be adding additional burdens to the present burdens of its people. Whatever gold we have in excess of what we need for the sciences and arts, we can dispose of for such articles of commerce as we actually require, and it will be that much to our advantage as against the present practice of hoarding it. We have more gold than any other nation, and if we cease to monetize it, the other nations will soon do the same. The common intelligence of the people generally has reached a point where they ought to take the lead in forwarding a plan

which will prove the use of any commodity as
legal tender to be a fallacy, and result in the
eventual discontinuance of such a practice.
America should lead in doing this.

Let us consider in concrete form the effect
that the money-loaners' dollars (which, by the
way, are the dollars that we use) have on the
cost of things,—and when I say cost, I mean the
expenditure, in human toil, necessary to acquire
the necessaries, conveniences, advantages and
luxuries appropriate to human life. I shall not
burden anyone with detailed figures, because a
mere statement will satisfy those who are sufficiently interested to study the present practices in the light of their own observation and
experience. I have examined the table of prices
of various staple articles for a period covering
forty-five years and have come to the conclusion
that the money loaners' dollar is not a measure
fitted to the requirements of a people desiring
equitable relations between each other. It is
simply a gambling dollar, and prices are regulated by a manipulation of it instead of by the
intrinsic value the commodities possess as
articles of necessity. The people who are engaged in useful occupations producing commod-

ities or serving other necessary demands of society are prevented from making the natural interchange of their products and services, because of the injection into their commerce of a fake currency and banking system, by the use of which speculators and financiers, so called, are able to pillage on all the exchanges. The system built up by these pillagers is an unnatural and unjust one.

It often happens that the aggregate value in money of a large quantity of a useful commodity will command less in one year than that of a smaller quantity brought in another year. Who, for instance, will claim that 3,000,000,000 bushels of wheat (supposing that to be the world's crop) is worth less in the aggregate for food and seed than 2,700,000,000 bushels, other things being equal, except money, which seldom is? No one claims that 3,000,000,000 bushels of wheat is actually worth less than 2,700,000,000. It is a fact, however, that the lesser quantity will often sell for as much, and sometimes more, than the larger quantity. A difference of ten cents a bushel will accomplish that result, if the 3,000,-000,000 sold for 90 cents and the 2,700,000,000 sold for one dollar. Illustrative of that fact, let me quote the following from *The Saturday Evening Post* of March 15, 1913:

"THE VICIOUS CIRCLE.

"We harvested bumper crops last year, you remember. May wheat at Chicago is worth ten cents a bushel less than a year ago; corn and oats about fifteen cents less. Yet commodity prices, as a whole, have declined scarcely at all. The index number, which compounds the price of many leading articles, is almost as high as ever, which means the cost of living is still about at the top notch.

The bumper crops stimulated trade in many lines —and that usually brings higher prices; while wheat went down, iron and steel products went up. What you saved on flour you lost on the pan to bake it in. And Wall Street echoes with complaints that investors, spurred on by higher cost of living, are demanding more interest, thereby raising the cost of manufacturing and transportation. This higher cost must be offset by higher prices, to overcome which investors must demand still more interest.

"Meanwhile labor, so to speak, chases its own tail, demanding higher wages, which result in higher prices that consume the increased wages—which naturally induces a demand for still higher wages that result in still higher prices."

Every farmer knows that a difference of ten cents a bushel between the price a commodity brings in one year and the price it brings the following year is not uncommon, but the railways charge full price for shipping every bushel, and the larger the crop the more they get, while the farmer must handle the additional wheat and get less for it. A farmer having the equivalent of 300 bushels of wheat to sell in a year when crops are generally abundant expects to receive a little less per bushel than he would receive per bushel for 270 bushels in a year when crops were not abundant, but he does not expect to give away the 30 bushels difference because he has more wheat than the year before. If that were to be the result, it would pay him, from his own individual financial standpoint, to burn up a part of his crop, when it was abundant. In fact, the cotton farmers of the south started to do that a few years ago when there was a large crop, and the price was very low. If the credit of the people had been coined into their own money instead of into the money-loaners' money, no thought of so destructive a nature would ever have occurred to the cotton growers or to any other producer of commodities.

In order to have a true measure of value we require a commercial measure regulated by the service value of things. That would mean a natural exchange as distinguished from our present artificial one. To make gold legal tender is artificial and not natural. It is because it is given an artificial value that it can be manipulated by the speculators against the general welfare. If the Government would supply storage facilities and accept for storage such products as could be practically and successfully stored and preserved, and then issue certificates of ownership to the owners therefor, these certificates would automatically equalize with each other and keep prices adjusted to natural conditions if they all formed a basis on which loans could be secured. The owner of gold, for example, would be given a certificate stating the amount and fineness of gold he had deposited and that he could secure its return upon the presentation of the certificate. Take an example from the present practice with relation to gold. At the close of business February 18, 1913, there were government gold certificates outstanding for $1,085,902,189, representing $880,741,390 gold coin and $205,160,779 gold bullion. These certificates are being circulated as money and the holders of them can secure the gold at any time they desire to present the certificates. The only thing that is wrong about that practice is that the gold is made legal ten-

der by the Government. Any other serviceable
commodity capable of practicable preservation
should have equal rights with gold. But none
should be monetized—made legal tender—
because whatever is monetized has an artificial
advantage.

Let us note a few things which would unquestionably forecast a betterment of conditions to
be brought about through the establishment of
an exchange system based upon commercial
value regulated by the service value of things.
For example, take ten commodities, gold, silver,
wheat, corn, cotton, rice, wool, iron, wood
in its various forms, and one more commodity
selected by yourself, to complete the ten. Let
us assume that this tenth commodity is your
own industrial product, whether it is labor or
whatever it may be. Now, let us see how these
will work in conjunction with each other on a
measure of their commercial service. Before
doing that, however, in order to clearly fix the
control, we should think for a moment about the
way in which the prices of these commodities
are now regulated by the money loaners'
dollars.

The money owner lets you have his dollars

created on your own credit, and he charges you interest which in a few years doubles his principal. In 100 years at the rate of 6%, the principal grows from $1 to $340. If the rate of interest be increased to 7, 8, 9 or 10% (which is not an uncommon rate for farmers and others to pay in new sections of the country) the accumulated interest, over a period of time, must necessarily be enormously greater. (See interest table in chapter on Interest, Dividends and Rent.) We do not have to live a hundred years, however, to get the practical results of the present financial system. We already have it in the form of an increased cost of living. Our present system has been in operation in its most aggravated form for more than fifty years, and we are now bearing a large part of the burden which it creates. Most of us have erroneously believed that the tariff is principally to blame, while in reality it is the financial system, and we cannot avoid its results whether we borrow money and pay interest or receive or pay money in selling and buying goods, and what is more, we will continue to get the same results as long as we allow the speculators and the financiers to use the same system. If you are a capitalist yourself, your advantages by reason of that fact will offset your disadvantages, and still leave you a balance on which to tax the rest of us, and you may thank the present piratical banking and currency system for it.

Let us now revert to our consideration of the establishment of a system of exchange based upon commercial value regulated by the service value of commodities, as well as the service value of the labor expended in the production and in the establishment of those things necessary to our common welfare. We will suppose that legal tender money is used when it is necessary to liquidate taxes, judgments, and other obligations of a character requiring the use of legal tender, and that in that case it is supplied by a government which coins its own credit—that is, the credit of the people—and pays it out for services rendered to the Government, and loans when that may seem necessary for the general welfare. This legal tender could and would be used generally.

In order to provide an index as a basis on which to establish values, let us divide the commodities before referred to into numbers and

assume that the general requirements of gold
and silver are 100 each; wheat, corn, cotton,
rice, wool, iron, and wood 10,000 each—a total
of 70,200, and labor 70,200, or equal to all of the
others (since it is practically responsible for
their production in serviceable form). I do not,
of course, claim that the relative demand for the
commodities and services is in the proportion
named by the figures, nor that the prices of each
would be the same, because there would
naturally be a difference in their service value,
as well as in the cost of their production.
I use these figures merely to illustrate the principle, and have left out land, as I wish to consider that by itself. Let us further assume that
the figures named represent the normal demand,
and that each represents a service to mankind
that corresponds to his demand. If this were
all true these commodities would, as long as
their production holds the same ratio, command
prices in the same proportion to their relative
cost of production. Certificates of storage
could be issued upon them. The holders, as
long as the certificates were unencumbered,
could transfer the title and secure proper prices
for them from those who were in need of the

commodities represented by the certificates, but if they did not sell, and found it necessary to have money, these certificates would also furnish the basis on which the government could issue loans, legal tender of government issue, in case of demand. I think, however, that we would discover before long that very few loans would be necessary. If they were they would, in effect, create asset currency instead of credit currency. Asset currency would properly belong to the party owning the assets, and he would be required to pay the Government for making it currency. Credit currency belongs to the people as a body. It is this failure to use the principles governing the two kinds of currency, in the practical operations of commerce and trade and in the functions of government, that renders our whole social system a false one. There would be no tariff problem at all if we had a proper financial system.

There should be no legal tender other than that issued by the Government, and no individual ought to be able to obtain it without giving its equivalent in return. If such were the case the problem of interest (as a disturbing factor) would cease, and a new era would dawn upon the world. The present difficult problems created by our arbitrary and ridiculous banking and currency system would then give place to natural selection. I use the term "natural selection" in its scientific sense, because we cannot run the Government in the interest of the people unless we follow the supreme laws that will unquestionably govern in the end. When we do there will be no choking up of the system by the arbitrary acts of the financial kings, for they are but a product of the arbitrary and unnatural practices that the people have fallen into the habit of using as a means of conducting their business, nor will the majority of men be paying penalties in the form of over-work, worry, and discouragement.

In order that we may understand more clearly the practical working out of the proposed new system, let us revert to our nine commodities—plus labor. To labor we have given the figure 70,200, to gold and silver 100 each, and to the others 10,000 each, making the total of the commodities 70,200, or equal to those of labor's products. Labor is not in the ordinary sense a commodity, but is superior, and a service of the highest order. In order to make our statement clear, we may as well distinguish it by its true name—labor. Suppose the nine commodities, at some one time, all fall ten points short of being sufficient to supply the demand. The owners of those commodities would of course demand higher prices, but the shortage would increase the demand for labor in order to bring the amount of the commodities produced up to the normal. In such a contingency the price of labor and the price of the nine commodities would all increase, and as between these ten, it would simply be a problem of increasing the production to the normal demand. Assuming that other things were normal, the greatest activity would prevail in the production of the nine, and the natural order would be to bring the amount of these up to the normal, and consequently would create a demand for labor. After that investment would follow. It would draw from among the other fields of production, and the equilibrium would be secured. The increased demand for labor, on which production depends, would enable those who worked to draw higher wages, and thus help to overcome the effect of the increased cost of the nine commodities. On the other hand, those who chose to remain idle, and those who engaged in other fields of labor, but who required the commodities in which the shortage continued, would find the cost of living to them increased as long as the shortage continued, but as we have just observed, if we were to adjust to the supreme law of natural selection, the equilibrium would quickly be secured.

Let us take another illustration. We will say that the production of the nine commodities is raised ten points above the normal. At such a time the prices would relatively decrease on all, and since the supply would be greater than the demand, less labor would be required in their production until the supply of these articles again became normal. When a system of exchange is established which is based upon service value instead of on credit and fiat, as it is under the present system, all parties supplying the things in general demand will be prepared for such a contingency, because under that system there will always be enough demand for their products to make all of the industrious prosperous. It does not, however, happen in actual experience that all things increase or decrease relatively the same in their production or demand. Consequently, their prices measured with each other will vary relatively with the varying production and demand. Under the system of exchange which I suggest, prices will automatically adjust to the existing conditions, because whenever there is a shortage or excess in the amount of an article of necessity, that article will advance or decrease in price in the proportion of its shortage or excess, and therefore enlist more energy when a shortage occurs and less when there is an excess in order to bring the amount produced to the normal. That is true even under the present system, but with the money placed in the arbitrary control of the money loaners the principal loss falls on the plain producers and consumers because of the monopoly control of money and credit. Under an exchange system regulated by service value and not by the money loaners, the increased or decreased cost created by the demand for the articles that are scarce or plentiful at the time would be consistent with the general supply of all things. For instance, when other things were normal, there would be no such thing as the aggregate money value of a large crop being less than the aggregate value of a small crop.

Everything would automatically and equably adjust in so far as it is possible for anything of human creation to do so.

The illustrations that I have given serve only to familiarize us with the principles involved. I desire to carry these into a somewhat more concrete form by taking examples from conditions that occur in actual production and consumption. Still using our nine commodities as our index, and including labor as the tenth, let us suppose that wheat falls short ten points in production, thus making the per unit demand sharper. That being a food product and the supply of and demand for food products being normally the same otherwise, all food products would rise in price when measured with all other commodities in which the demand and supply remained normal, because wheat being the commodity in which the shortage occurred, other food products would be required to take its place as food. Therefore, wheat, corn, and rice would all cost more per unit than they had before and wheat would cost the most. The result would be that these cereal foods would be worth more per unit when measured with the commodities in which there was no shortage in the amount produced. As measured with the commodities which we have considered, we will merely say as an illustration, that, when all are considered commercially the shortage in the amount of the cereal wheat would decrease from the normal 10,000 to 9,500, but while with the stronger demand the total decrease in price value would not be equal to the decrease in the volume, it would demand more per bushel but less for the whole crop. The extra necessity of supplying the food loss in wheat would cause the cereals rice and corn, which remained normal in volume, 10,000 each, to exceed the normal in their price value, and we will say that they would raise in value from 20,000, their total normal price, to 20,500, and thus, as between the three cereals named, the result would be that the 9,000 wheat would command 9,500 of the commercial value, whereas when the value was 10,000 normal, the normal price was 10,000 while the 20,000 corn and rice, normal in quantity but sharper in demand to make up for the food loss in wheat, would command 20,500 in commercial value. It naturally follows that the commercial value of

the three cereals measured with each other
alone, would total the same, or 30,000, but the
food supply would be short 1,000 bushels of
wheat. The commercial food supply would be
that much short or less valuable in any true
measure, and as measured with the amount of
all commodities, respectively, their value would
be short and would not command the normal—
30,000 in price, but the unit price of all three
cereals would be higher. There would follow
an immediate demand upon the farmers to
make up the supply of wheat. The increased
price of that commodity would cause the greatest effort to be applied to its production. The
demand would adjust the amount of production (of course, assuming natural conditions for
raising wheat about the same). The same would
be true of a decrease of or increase in any other
of the commodities. But, the moment you
monetize the metals gold and silver, these being
commodities that are peculiarly under the control of but a few persons, an arbitrary condition is created and the equilibrium is immediately destroyed. Then the artificial demand
for the gold and silver gives to its owners the
power to manipulate the prices of all the other

commodities in their own selfish interests, and
to make this worse, the Government has delegated to the money loaners the privilege of
coining the people's credit and selling that to
the people, thus practically forcing them to buy
it in order to carry on the business of the country.

The reader will not be misled by my use of
certain commodities as a means of illustrating
the principles involved in our study. I use them
only for that purpose, and the reader himself
must develop a method of his own if he wishes
to go into further details on that point. My
purpose is to show that our present system is in
error, which I have already done, and also to
show that it cannot be amended so as to make it
a good system. I believe I have shown that
also. We can, however, make such amendments
as will render it practicable for us to use it
preliminary to the establishment of an entirely
new system based upon a plan which will serve
the true purposes of exchange. We shall have
to provide the latter before our social relations
can even approximate social justice.

All mentally well-balanced persons know that
we are not governed by the true principles of

social justice when we make the main aim of our social existence the gaining of money. Such a condition of action has resulted from the use of a false money standard,—a gambling standard. I think we realize this and are therefore prepared for the most important part of our study,—the actual study of a system which will straighten out our social tangles.

The principal reason for the general scramble and scrap for money is that it is hard for those who need it the most to get it. As long as the people generally are in dire need of it, and but a few of the people control it, this scrap and scramble will continue to the loss of the many and the gain of the few, but if we establish a system that will make it easy for the industrious to obtain money by means of their applied labor, or other valuable thing to give in return or as security for it, we shall remove the gambling element from money, and the general scramble for it (simply in order to control it) will cease,—cease, because every person will know that it may be had when he needs it if he can return value for it. The inducement will then be for all to get into a position to be able to provide a product for exchange purposes, and instead of having a lot of speculating parasites, we shall have men and women who are willing to enter into useful, practical industry of the highest and most economic order, because at all times properly applied industry may obtain money when it is needed. Of course it would not absolutely destroy speculation and gambling in money because money would unquestionably have value, and, therefore, people who did not care to earn it would speculate to get it without if they could, but industrious people would be independent because they could get money in return for their own industry, and they would not be compelled to deal with the speculators as they now are. Neither the farmer, the wage earner, nor other persons engaged in performing a service of general value, would be compelled to pay a rate of interest that, in and of itself, destroys his efficiency as an independent person. When money primarily serves the purpose of facilitating exchanges it will be serving its true purpose. Then any one should be able to get it who can return value for it, and primarily the Government must fill the office of furnishing it.

Stating the same thing in another way, in or-

der to reach the same conclusions from a different viewpoint, money should simply serve to
make exchanges, and be cancelled when it has
fulfilled its purpose the same as checks are used
and cancelled. When a person does not wish to
make an exchange he needs no money, and will
care for none if he knows that he can secure it
readily when he needs it. The bankers are now
supplying that service by means of the clearing
of checks. These checks serve as a kind of
money, but unless you can deposit the actual
money with your banker, you must make terms
with him in order to be able to draw checks on
his bank. If you are financially responsible he
will make you a loan. You give him your note
and he will credit you on his bank books with
the amount of your note. But the price he
charges you makes the accommodation too expensive, and therefore the fact that the banks
furnish that accommodation, does not remove
the element of speculation nor the desire on
the part of the people generally to secure money
simply for the satisfaction of having it. When
one has money he can use it without paying
someone else for its use, and while he is not
using it he can loan it and charge the borrower

according to the same interest method that the banks use, but with this difference;—the banker can loan mere credit when the borrower himself is good for the credit. The bank makes the borrower's credit merchantable by accepting and honoring it in the borrower's checks, but individuals can loan actual money only.

The bankers have a true system of clearing exchanges. As an example of that I call attention to the fact that in 1911 there was cleared through the one hundred and forty Clearing House Associations $92,420,120,092. There scheme is a good one for taking care of the exchanges of the country and it helps the country as long as we have not a better one. By its use only $47.80 of actual cash is required in order to handle each $1,000,000 (of checks on the banks) that passes through the clearing houses. But unfortunately for us, the fees the bankers charge for putting our own credit on their books, before we are even enabled to draw checks, is so great that the people generally are over-burdened by reason of it. That is shown in the chapter on "Interest, Dividends and Rents."

Of course these exchanges should go on wherever they serve the general welfare, and since we ourselves have not provided a better method, we are under obligations to the bankers for having honored and made current and merchantable our own credit. But since these exchanges relate to our business and are used directly by most of us at some time, and indirectly by all of us all of the time, we should establish a system that will give us the least costly service. The main thing for us to do is to eliminate most of the interest charges and make it practicable for the human family to thrive by industry, by having industry available to all people who wish to be and are industrious. That does not mean that the banks should be superceded by new exchange agents, but it does mean that the banks should be required to adjust to a new system that will cost the people less. It means also that there would be fewer banks, because under any economic system of exchange there would be no more necessity for several banks in cities of less than ten or twenty thousand people than there would be a need for several post-offices in towns of that size.

Let us take up the discussion from still another viewpoint in order that no one shall possibly misunderstand. Money as such is not a thing of prime necessity. It is merely a convenience which enables us to make such exchanges as we may wish without the cumbersome handling of property. It is comparable to a due bill that is due to the holder from a person having something to sell which the owner of the money desires to have. The money is turned over to the owner of the property or to the person rendering a service after which the latter becomes the owner of the money. That is, the due bill, which is collectible again from any other person who has property to sell or service to render that the holder of the money or due bill may wish to buy.

The banks have taught us to use checks instead of the actual money, and it is true that they cash these, but, as we observed before, we cannot draw checks until we have arranged with our banker, and in order to make that arrangement, unless we have the real money, we must pay him interest at a rate that makes the greatest number of men poor and a few enormously rich. The fact that the bankers can make exchanges that represent hundreds of billions of dollars annually, when, as a matter of fact, there never was at any one time as much

as $1,700,000,000 in all of the banks combined
(and of the money they do actually hold which
is approximately $1,500,000,000, two-thirds of it
or more is lying dead in their vaults as reserves
and is never used).

We are under obligation to the banks for
teaching us this economy in the use of money
and credit. But after all, as we observed before, the credit is supported and maintained by
the resources of the people and the daily application of their energy. The banks have simply
filled the office of making it current and merchantable. We do not owe that tribute to the
bankers, and thanking them for the good that
they have done, but for which they have been
well and even over paid, we are now prepared
as a people in our national capacity to pass the
necessary laws, and to perform the governmental function laid down by the Constitution,
"To coin money, regulate the value thereof"
(and "of Foreign coin" when used in our country), in behalf of all the people of these United
States. We should profit by the example of the
banks in copying somewhat after some parts of
the system they have used for making exchanges, but as a Government we ought to fur-

nish the advantage to all of the people on equality and with the least expense practicable. The Government can do what the banks are doing and save to the people as much as the banks make in excessive dividends, besides the still greater profits that are made on speculation on the side.

The Government shall "coin money and regulate the value thereof." That is the Constitutional provision. The great special interests have been sticklers for following the Constitution whenever it has blocked the way to the people's progress if that might in any way interfere with the practice of the interests, but whenever the special interests find it to their advantage to follow any practice profitable to them, the fact that such practice may be in contravention to the Constitution and the laws does not in the least embarrass or hinder them, as long as the people do not invoke the law. When the people do, every possible dilatory tactic is resorted to by the interests to delay compliance. The consequence has been that the Constitution has often been used as an instrument of obstruction to prevent the people from enforcing their rights.

Now, I have called attention to the absolute right and sovereign power vested in the people themselves, to "coin money and regulate the value thereof." No Constitutional amendment is required to be adopted by three-fourths of the States. It can be done right now, and why delay?

What I am proposing will cause such a howl to come from the special interests as has not been heard for a very long time. The "stand-pat" press will jump into the breach for them, and howl for "sound money"—the money that "sounds" good to them, because of their special interest. When you see the "standpat" papers doing that, go back a few pages in this book and read the circulars,—Quotations "B," "C," "D" and "E." Then give such credit to the howl as you believe it to be entitled to. No! it is too late now for them. This time they brought "the last straw," and we caught them before they were able to put it on us. "Sound Money" will be the song that will be sung to you by every advocate of the special interests. I have shown, and they have already stated and proved, that what they have in the past called "sound money" is not "sound."

By doing that they save me the trouble of inserting herein a chapter of evidence that I had gathered to prove what they now admit. By that admission they disclose the fact, and it is a fact, that they have defrauded all of the people by their so-called "sound money." Their kind of sound money has enabled them to become wealthy and independent, but it has prevented the people generally from doing what they have a right to do and should have done, namely: retained the fruits of their own labor.

The kind of exchange that we should use is the kind that anybody who has value to give can get without paying usury. That kind will be the sound money of the people—the honest money. Those who wish gold may have it—there will be nothing to prevent their buying it. We, the people, on their presenting it, will stamp its weight and fineness for anyone who will pay the costs of doing so. We will do that to insure to the people who wish the gold the amount the Government stamp certifies that there is in any given piece of the metal. That is honest, and to do anything more is dishonest to the people, but the Government could not say that it was legal tender and thereby give it a special quality that it did not possess in itself. We can do the same with any commodity that it is practicable to use as a thing of exchange. The demand for commodities of all kinds will be in proportion to the service they may render to the people and no one should complain when absolute justice is to be done. As a consequence the Government would create no more "commodity" money, either for itself or for the people, because it would not only be unjust to do so but unnecessary and ridiculous. When anyone wishes commodities let them buy them as such.

Everybody knows that we must have some money, and now the question arises as to what kind it shall be. "Honest money," of course, instead of what we have now and are told is "sound money," whereas in truth it is the opposite of "Honest money," and should have been named accordingly. We want a kind of money the buying and selling properties of which remain respectively constant. In other words, we want a kind of money that will buy the exact equivalent of what it cost us to get it. We want the kind of money that serves the same office among the people in their commercial and social relations with each other as the drafts and checks serve in the business transactions entered into by the bankers. We do not intend that the bankers shall have a better system for themselves than we have for ourselves. We expect to pay those whose duty it will be to help make the exchanges. The bankers will be able to give as effective and valuable service in this other up-to-date system as they have given us heretofore, but the past service has been altogether too expensive and therefore not sufficiently effective. We have no prejudice to vent upon the bankers. As the system stands they serve the people, generally, the best they can. There are always, of course, a few isolated exceptions. But the time for us to do for ourselves what the bankers are doing for themselves, is here and now, and we should hasten to adopt a system of exchange under which it will cost the people no more to make their commercial exchanges between each other than it costs the banks to make exchanges between the bankers and their cash customers. It is just as simple for us as it is for them, and we have the indisputable right. We owe it to ourselves, to our children, and to all posterity to have an efficient, self-sustaining, and effective system.

The people are the Government. Therefore the Government should, as the Constitution provides, regulate the value of money. There is no other real sovereign power, because all authority emanates from the people. Money is the means of exchange among all people. Its regulation is absolutely a governmental function, and the Government has no natural inherent power that enables it to impart to money any other property or quality than that of making it the agent of exchange. Let us see how that could be done if we were to apply the principles that should govern.

Every dollar that the Government must pay is collected from the people themselves. In other words, they pay for it. When the Government spends $1,000,000,000 it collects $1,000,000,000. It spends and collects more than that amount annually. It collects it from the people and pays it out to individuals from whom it is presumed that it gets the equivalent in value for what it spends. To say that it does get an equivalent in value is a very violent presumption under present conditions; for, however true the presumption is legally, it is far from the truth in practice. Let us study that statement a little.

A "middle-man" slipped into this game. I term it a game because he got in, for that is what it amounts to. The "middle-man" is the money loaner and banker. The Government pays the $1,000,000,000 which it has collected from itself—that is, from the people. A considerable sum included in that is interest. This interest is paid to the "middle-man," but for the Government to pay interest is an absurdity. After an analysis of that statement we will be compelled to admit that the payment of interest by the Government is an absurdity.

We can easily understand the true meaning of exchange, and at the same time the true purpose of money, if we use the business of the Government itself as an example. For convenience rather than for exactness of the sum (although it is approximately correct) we will say that the Government pays out every ten or eleven months $1,000,000,000 and collects that sum from itself; that is, from the people, in approximately an equal period of time. That is virtually what happens. Now, will someone in all of these United States tell the people why the Government—the people—pay interest on such a simple proposition? They get the service, or whatever it may be that is to be paid for, and tax themselves to pay for it, but they add to the tax a sum of interest, and for that they get no consideration.

Suppose the Government should issue its legal tender notes to those performing services or furnishing material to the Government. These notes would draw no interest, but they would be legal tender. A person who performed a service for which the Government owed him $50 would get this legal tender in payment. It might be a $50 certificate or ten of $5 each, or some other amount, if desired. The certificates would be proof that the bearer had given the service and that the people had certified to it and therefore owed it. The way to pay the tax, for that is what it amounts to, would be to get these certificates and in order to do that we would have to pay for them in the goods or services we had for sale that the bearer might be in need of. These certificates would be obtained by those owing taxes and tendered to the Government in payment. They would be in demand generally for the very

reason that that could be done. One transaction
would cancel the other and the certificates
would be cancelled as rapidly as they were ten-
dered to the Government in payment of taxes,
on exactly the same principle that men deposit
their earnings in banks and draw checks on
the accounts, and the checks are cancelled by
the banks when paid. It is as simple as A, B, C.
The banks are carrying on this system among
themselves and those who deposit cash at a very
small cost, a business that is "on all fours" exactly on that principle. Therefore, I repeat, let
us profit by the example of the banks. Let us
call them in to serve us on the true principles
of exchange and pay them for the value of their
services, but not permit them to be our masters
in the world of commerce nor to appropriate as
a private enterprise for selfish purposes, or for
any purpose at all, the functions that are properly those belonging to the Government itself.
Let the Government issue all the legal tender
and circulate it (but without the necessity of
indorsement), according to the present manner
of the passing of checks between the customers
of banks and the banks themselves.

I have already shown in the chapter on "Interest, Dividends and Rents'' that our system of finance is ''self-extinguishing,'' whereas it should be ''self-sustaining.'' No one with intelligence can honestly deny the truth of that statement. This chapter is designed to show how a system of finances may be made self-sustaining and also how to adopt a financial system that will give us a money that will command as an article of purchase an amount equivalent to what it cost us to get the money. In the last paragraph the true principle is exemplified in regard to the business that is to be transacted between the Government and the people in their individual capacity. The people have business with each other individually in which the Government has no share or direct interest. These are private transactions and for the handling of these there is also required a convenient means of exchange. The same principle that underlies the transactions between the Government and the people in their individual capacity underlies the transactions between individuals privately, with this difference: the Government is the sovereign power and the citizens the sovereigns, and therefore through their sovereign power (the Government) they may create the money that facilitates the exchange, but may not do so when they deal with each other, because each is a sovereign with no authority over the other. Therefore, they must act collectively—that is, by their sovereign power when fixing the medium of exchange.

Now we must not forget that money is a mere representative. In its true purpose it is like a tax, as the illustration in our last paragraph shows. But when it is used and applied to transactions between individuals it becomes voluntary in so far as such things can. The citizen will not lose sight of the fact that every service merits the return of an equal service. The laborer should receive the value of his labor, and the employer the value of the service he renders. The party who was served obtained the results and should pay for them in all cases. He should pay for them with an amount of money that represents an equal service given by him to the party from whom he got it, and that party again should have given an equal value and so on. Now, while it is not possible to have the deals between individuals work out with such absolute justice as the statement contemplates for the basic law, the basis for the

medium of exchange should be on that absolutely just basis. God has created man according to
a consistent principle. The failure of men to
measure up with each other on an equal plane
physically, mentally and spiritually is not due
to a failure of the principles of Creation. So,
too, laws which men have made for government
in the interest of the general welfare, should be
made according to a consistent principle, in
order that no indictment shall lie against the
law because men fail in the practical application
of it to measure the transactions between them
with absolute justice. Co-lateral laws may be
provided to remedy the infractions as far as
possible. . We can come the nearest to securing
justice in our social relations if the basic law is
right, and in this problem of money the law
should be based on the principle of simple exchange, the giving of an equivalent for its
equivalent, which is absolutely impossible under
our present laws. In fact, our laws now nega-
tive any such possibility and our social evils
cannot be remedied as long as they stand as
they are now. The only true and honest course
for the people themselves to take is to go directly to the roots of the evil and devise a sys-

tem of financial laws which shall be based upon the true principles.

All commodities, including gold and silver, are purely and naturally articles of commerce, and their respective owners have the right to receive such return for their exchange as their respective values measure in other commodities or money according to the agreement of the parties so dealing. Because gold generally, and silver in some instances, have been made legal tender the whole system of social intercourse has gone far astray from the true road which leads to the highest progress of which men are capable.

There is no remedy for the social evils in the standardization of any commodity as a dollar. No commodity can be made an honest standard for money. No honest money can exist except that which is representative, which must be the Government dollar. It must be the representative of exchange only. Any other action that may be taken will not stand long because the present increasing general intelligence will render that impossible, and it will cost the people dearly while it does stand, in exactly the same way that we are paying now for what was wrongly made the standard heretofore. We have already noted the principles that should truly govern in the transactions entered into by the Government and the people in their individual capacities. We have seen that every dollar to be paid by the Government for a service rendered to it is to be collected in the form of some tax from the people. The principles naturally governing the exchanges between individuals rests upon the same principle as that governing the exchanges between the Government and individuals. One transaction presumably offsets the corresponding related transactions. But in the transactions of government there is no element of commercialism. The Government is not in business for profit, and presumably, it does those things only that are necessary in order to maintain an effective government. It needs what it buys, and there is nothing left over that it does not require for the use of the Government. But it is otherwise with individuals. They transact business, and work for profits as well as to maintain their existence. That may be stated as a general rule, for there are very few who do not seek in some way to stack up a fortune, notwithstanding that comparatively few are successful. But some are successful, and these have an excess over and above what they require for their ordinary existence. What they have in excess of what is necessary for their ordinary requirements is extra. That is what we call capital—what is left over after all of their other exchanges are complete.

Now as long as we recognize capital to be consistent with our social existence, in principle, we shall have to recognize it as separate and removed from the ordinary exchanges. As soon as a person has more than he can use, and more than it is necessary for him to sell as a means of securing money with which to buy what he wishes to use, and puts that excess on the market for the sole purpose of obtaining money without intending to use the money in exchange for some necessary or desired commodity or service, he retires that much money from serving its true purpose. Money created for the purposes of exchange should be in constant activity. It should be issued as rapidly as needed and retired as rapidly as used, somewhat on the principle governing the use of checks, but the Government should serve as the issuing agent in the case of money

I think the statements I have made thus far show the distinction between the Government paying for its purchases or for services rendered to it on the one hand, and on the other the dealings of individuals with each other. In the case of the Government the dealings are absolutely cancelled. That is, the Government pays a dollar and it must collect a dollar in return. It acquires no capital as the term is ordinarily understood. It can issue a currency for its purposes with absolute consistency without ever paying a dollar of interest. In fact, it is inconsistent for it to do otherwise, because its business should be on the basis of pure exchange—a service to the people and a tax to pay the cost of the service. In the dealings of individuals with each other, capital must be taken into consideration in our calculations. Therefore in the settlement of this problem it will be more difficult to deal with private exchanges than with the exchanges that take place between the Government and individuals.

I therefore advocate a commodity exchange that may be used to relieve the burdens that capital places upon the current exchanges that take place from day to day in the commerce that is a result of the daily activities of men and the necessities of life. The commodity exchange may be selected by the capitalist himself according to his own wishes. If he wishes gold, the Government, on being paid the cost of the process, could certify to the weight and fineness of such as shall be presented. The same could be done with any other article that is capable of being treated in a like manner. Then the capitalist could use whatever it might be in trade if he liked. It could be passed from one to another, but it would not be termed dollars nor would it be legal tender. It would be designated by its weight and would stand on its own merits. Its value in true money would depend on the service it rendered in supplying the real needs of men.

The actual money could be issued by the Government in order to facilitate exchange. Its value ought to be fixed by the Government as the Constitution provides, after which it should pass current as checks now do, but with this exception: the makers of checks can be known to only a very limited number of persons, while the

Government is known to all, and therefore the
Government money should pass for full credit
with all people. All of the money that business
demanded would be supplied and the purpose
of the money would be to steady and equalize
the prices of all commodities and services so
that those engaged in any kind of enterprise,
work or occupation that was of service to humanity might be enabled to command their
share in the proportion of the demand for the
service performed. No greater sums of money
would be required to carry on the natural commerce, as distinguished from the present speculative commerce, than it would be necessary
for the producers to use in exchanging the surplus of their particular kind of products for
other kinds of products that they might require
and that were the products of other producers.
It would not change the general practice of paying with checks. The money would be deposited in the banks and checked on in the same
way that it is done now. The banks would serve
as the clearing agencies and would be paid for
their services as such. They would, however,
be compelled to adjust to a new basis. Under
such a system they would not be our masters

nor would they be in control of the industrial and social conditions of the country, but would simply be our equals. Then all people could act on an independent basis. Money would no longer be hoarded, but would be kept in motion because no more would be issued than was reasonably required. If all people having the industry or the means could secure it when it was needed, the aim and ideals of life would not be governed by the dollar. Production and not speculation would control the material conditions of men. All men would then be on an equality in so far as that is possible, and the incentive would be toward becoming truly industrious instead of toward becoming speculative parasites. After that the modern inventions and new methods of application that so immensely increase the productive capacity of the people generally would inure to the general welfare, instead of centralizing into a few hands the products of men's activity and allowing it to be made the basis on which to compound interest dividends and profits by the rule of geometrical progression and ultimately levied as a toll upon the people generally.

THE PRACTICAL SIDE OF A BETTER FINANCIAL SYSTEM.

Those who are accustomed to deal with social problems from the standpoint of true basic principles as well as from the standpoint of what is in common practice in politics, business and social intercourse, will find sufficient in the foregoing chapters to outline the coming changes that are inevitable to the ultimate control of the financial dealings of men. It does not follow that the changes will take place at once. In fact, plans have already been made by the special interests and bills have been drafted and are ready for an early adoption, unless the people arise in opposition to these bills and in defense of their own rights. The truth is, the people cannot defend their own rights unless they awake generally to the importance of those rights, which will require a most careful study of the political, industrial and financial problems, and they are so much handicapped because of the great pressure that is placed upon them to eke out an existence under the present system that it is difficult for them to secure enough extra time to give to these problems the proper study. Men ought not, however, to be discouraged, because, with all the modern advantages and means of production, it is hard to understand how the people could get less than they do now, but if they continue to seek to become better informed, the future will be characterized by evidences of progression and not of reaction.

I have not set forth any bills in drafted form ready for enaction, because that is a mere detail which should come at a time when things have shaped themselves so as to make that step necessary. The ground must be plowed before the seeding is done. The people themselves must do the plowing. After that they must seed the land and keep possession of the field if they wish to harvest and reap the fruits of their labor. They have always done the plowing, the seeding, the cultivating, and practically all of the work in the field of industrial enterprise, but they have never reaped the results of their labor. There has always been a Rothschild, a Gould, a Rockefeller, a Carnegie, a Morgan and men of their kind, and a few thousand lesser harvesters who have gathered in the best fruits

out of the fields of industry. They are on hand
and active at every point of vantage. They
understand human selfishness and know how to
deal with the individuals whom the people have
selected to represent them. They know that the
individual citizen whose interest is the same as
that of the citizens in general, will not find it
practicable to spend the time, in the legislative
halls or in Congress, to exert a direct influence
over his official representative. But the other
parties to whom I have alluded send their representatives to influence the people's representatives, and the manner of their influence is
so varied in its application that no description
of its application in one case would serve as an
index to another. I shall deal with that particular phase of the subject on another occasion,
but before dropping it at this point, let me call
the attention of the citizen to the fact that he
must be on guard that the new progressive
spirit and movement is kept alive, and that the
special interests are made to understand that it
is alive. The special interests are more alert
individually than the people themselves are individually, for the reason that the interests get
the bulk of the wealth that grows out of the

work of the people, and, therefore, the special interests are seeking to convert the progressive movement into another victory for themselves.

I started as an original progressive when there were but a few on the battle line of progressiveness, and I had known the wily moves employed by the interests in their efforts to divert this progressive movement to their own advantage, not only in dividing the progressives into factions and parties, which means one and the same thing in its effect upon the people, but in what is worse than that, the attempt on their part to fill the ranks of the progressives with spies and traitors and then presume through selfish influence to convert many of those who honestly started the movement. "Temptation, thou art a mighty power in the hands of those who hold the seductive bait." The interests base their hope of victory upon the temptation furnished by that "bait." Their first hope was to win by ridiculing the progressives and taking patronage from those whom the people had elected, but this proved a failure.

The interests, ever alert to their purposes, selected from amongst their own attorneys and agents, and others willing to take their "bait," the most wily ones and posed them as progressives in order to meet the emergency forced on them by the progressive movement. These men advocated the progressive principles and, while still claiming to be progressives, became candidates for office, and are dangerous because they pass as one thing and are at heart something wholly different. That is now the principal danger that confronts the progressive movement. There is one way by which it may be overcome, and I have advocated it from the very start. Destroy all party government! In other words, let the people as a Nation govern, the same as, hereafter, Minnesota will have a legislature made up from and by the people as a whole and not from a faction as it has been hitherto. Congress at this time is an example of party government. A single party claims to usurp the powers and the rights of the people in general, and, what is more, they brazenly state that they have taken control as a party. That is only following the tracks in an old beaten path.

Several of the same things that I originally advocated as wise provisions for the people have now been adopted in my own State, Minnesota. One of these, and I emphasized it whenever an opportunity was presented, was to destroy party lines and unite the people in such a way that the interests could not whip us by their use of the boss system in the contest, and because of our separate divisions. I am proud to state that in the State of Minnesota, and it is the first State of which the statement can be made, a man can no longer run for a county office or for the Legislature and get the name of a party appendix affixed to his name on the official ballot. When I first advocated that, the stand-patters to a unit ridiculed me for it, but they were forced to yield because the people were determined to have it, and public sentiment is supreme.

To be a true Progressive it is not sufficient to stand up and say that one believes in what has been promulgated as progressive principles. One must be progressive in heart and active in promoting the progressive principles of today, tomorrow and always. There is no resting point, for humanity is ever ascending to a higher and better goal. All that has been promulgated thus far as political doctrines by the progressives would, if adopted *in toto,* be stand-pat tomorrow if the people were generally content to let it go at that. It is on that theory, and in the hope that that will happen, that so many agents from the special interests are being sent into the progressive ranks. They are willing to take an advance step if there is a hope that it can be stopped at that. But that is not the purpose of the true progressives. Their aim is to take step after step toward higher and nobler purposes and the general elevation of mankind. They recognize the advantages that God's Creation furnishes and the advantage that man's intelligence can make of the conditions existing. They propose to utilize these in every practical way as well as to supply the instruments and the means to create a better condition for the people generally. There is no monopoly of the principle by party or sect. It is open and free to anyone who wishes to embrace it, but if one becomes a party to a faction, even if the faction is called a party, and lets a majority of that faction take him away from the broader field of national activity, by that act he ceases to be a progressive.

Returning to our financial study. The citizen

who would acquire the greatest efficiency as a
citizen of a great commonwealth, and at the
same time consistently hold the individual independence that people generally are entitled to,
must realize that a new medium of exchange is
necessary. We must get away from the idea
that money is created to serve any other purpose than that of an exchange agent. As long
as it is used for any other purpose it does not
serve as a true exchange agent. If we want the
agent more than we want the substance it commands, our life activities become a gamble.
This we have already shown. Men generally
must be made to understand that property is
not produced to obtain money for it, but to
serve the general needs, and that money is
wholly a secondary matter created to facilitate
the exchange of the property and to bring the
producer into intimate relations with the consumer's needs. Under any well-regulated system the people generally would be consumers
and producers continually. We cannot educate
people in such a manner that they would have
no incentive to speculate if the opportunity was
presented or believed to offer profit. As long
as we have a speculators system the great

majority of us,—and I may as well say all, because the exceptions are very few,—will speculate if we think we can make a profit out of it. Therefore, it does no good to condemn the system alone. We shall have to appeal to the selfish side of our natures, and I use the word "selfish" in no faulty sense, because even selfishness may serve a good purpose, and in the sense in which I now use it, it would. Every citizen who does not enjoy a special privilege has a commendable selfish interest in destroying all special privileges because then he, and all other citizens similarly situated, would be very much more successful. Since that includes all but a very small fraction of all of the people, it is easy to understand that when it becomes generally known that the people would be almost infinitely more successful if they were to make certain political, industrial and financial changes, they will most certainly do so in their own "selfish" interest. I am appealing to this "selfish" interest as the best way in which to secure a reform of our political, industrial and financial relations. I am not pessimistic, but I know the inducement is sufficient to accomplish the end that is sought. It is on that account

that I would have all of the elements of inducement for speculation removed from our legal
tender money. It is because it is for the interest
of the people generally that I am sure it can be
accomplished through them as soon as they
realize the advantages they would procure as a
result of the change. Once it is made easy for
the industrious, and those who have the accumulated results of industry, to obtain money
when they need it in order to effect an exchange
of one kind for something of another kind, it
will be good-bye to the multi-millionaire and the
parasite. They will then become citizens who
will be given credit for what they can do that
is of worth to the general public. Then the true
conservation will be known, and it will be found
that the people may have very much more than
they now have with less than half the waste,
both in time and material.

Now, let us bear strictly in mind that there
would naturally be two kinds of exchange. One
a commodity exchange measured absolutely by
the relations of the commodities to each other
in the proportion of the demand and service for
them. That has already been explained. The
other would be the legal tender—the money

issued by the Government, which has already been partly explained. There would be no limit to the amount for which goods could be exchanged for other goods or services for other services. One can conceive that there might be combinations to "corner" certain commodities somewhat like the combinations that now take place, but the opportunity for such corners would be immensely reduced by the fact that there could be no corner in money which would be directly controlled by the people themselves through their Government. If something of which they were in need was cornered they would be free to start an industry for its immediate production, because the funds would be supplied. The truth is that no corners would occur for the very reason that the object for which corners are made would not be accomplished. Of course, perfection would not be attained, but immense improvement would be.

It will not be difficult for almost anyone to understand the manner in which commodities would exchange one for the other, and that gold or silver bullion might be used more or less as an agency of exchange, at least as long as other countries used it. But it is more difficult to understand how the legal tender, the real money, would be kept so that it could at all times be exchanged with about the same advantage and not be fluctuated in a way that would make its possessor uncertain as to what office it would perform for him if he had it on his hands for any considerable period of time.

One of the serious objections that I interpose to the present system is that people should wish to hoard money. It does not serve its place as money when it is hoarded. Its office is to serve as exchange and when it shall be used for that, and the Government (by which is understood all of the people) shall regulate its value as the Constitution provides, the general welfare will be to preserve the value of the exchange at as nearly a uniform standard, measured by the general average of prices, as it is possible to do under any system, and far better than it is being done under the present system. After that, if some people wish to hoard money, they may do so without its interfering with the commerce of the people. When it is taken from its hoarding quarters and put back into circulation it will relieve the pressure for the issue by the Government of that much money. There will be no inflation of prices because the comparative supply (service) of and demand for a commodity or service will determine its price instead of being controlled by those who monopolize money.

Of course, under a true system of exchange the interest problem will be almost eliminated. It should be, but the experts in dealing in exchange will continue because of the good service they can render. The banking business will still be a necessity to mankind, but instead of having all deals measured in interest terms, as they are now, there will be charges for the work done and the responsibility assumed. Property will not be monopolized by a few and given a status that is superior to personal rights, and sums of money and properties will not then perpetually offset in earning power the work and energy of human beings. This money and property will, of course, serve humanity as products of the prior industrial accumulation and therefore reduce the requirements for present production to the extent of the accumulation, and the owners would be able to take advantage of that fact and go off on a vacation if they cared to while they were consuming what they had received as a result of such an advantage. But they cannot set it aside and contract, with the Government backing such a contract, that the equivalent of each dollar should form the basis on which to extort compound interest from the present and future generations that should not and cannot be paid. Again I refer the reader back to the table of compound interest for a positive proof of the impossibility of continuing our present system.

I have not advocated in this volume anything that is impracticable. What I advocate is natural and just, but inasmuch as it differs from what we are accustomed to hearing sanctioned, it will be bitterly attacked by those who have the special advantages at the present time. They are in a position to make us trouble, because the system is so arbitrary that they can bring on a panic even if God's Glorious Creative Forces should respond to man's desires in a more bountiful way than ever before.

There are many things in connection with this great subject of Banking and Currency that I would discuss further in this volume if the interests were not urging the early adoption of the kind of banking and currency laws that they wish Congress to enact, and which would only favor them. I consider it necessary to put this volume out as rapidly as it can be done. I do that in the belief that at least in some measure it will result in reducing the number of the jokers that are certain to go through Congress in the next banking and currency bill that will be passed. I know enough about the situation here in Congress to be aware of the fact that the legislation that will be enacted will be favorable to the special interests. It may contain some "sop to the people," as the conniving politicians here in Washington state with a wink at each other, but it will not be a people's banking and currency measure that will be next adopted. There may be some compromise, and it may be better than what we now have, but the people are entitled to all that is due to them, and they will not get it from this Sixty-third Congress. If the people were to study and understand their rights, and elect men to represent them who understand and favor just and fair legislation, it would not be difficult to frame honest and just laws for the practical government of the financial dealings of the people. That could be done before the election of the

Sixty-fourth Congress, and that Congress could be elected for that purpose. I do not make that statement from the standpoint of any party, because I do not believe in the control of Congress by any party.

The present Congress is run by a caucus system and so long as that is done there is little chance of getting into a bill provisions that have not been approved by the bosses, because the bosses will only approve of things favorable to the people as a whole when they believe that the people themselves will fail to re-elect them if they do not. Under this present system of running Congress by a party caucus, the minority of the people are bound to rule. Even honest members, misguided by a false notion of party obligation, submit to the dictates of an unofficial caucus and become the tools of the boss system. No man should be re-elected to Congress who has entered into the councils of a caucus with the public excluded, unless he unequivocally promises never again to do so. In other words, no one should be left without hope if he reforms. Let him be ever so honest, and even very able, his submission to such an ordeal as a method of transacting public business is proof of his incapacity to appreciate the purposes for which the Government of the United States was organized—namely, to be run by the people in the interests of all of the people, and not as a party movement to be controlled by a faction of the people in the interests of a faction of the people.

This volume advises of many of the present inconsistencies in the practice of finances. I shall follow it later with a revision which will show how the farm and other credits should be provided for.

APPENDIX A.

The discussion of so important a problem as that of Banking and Currency will naturally cause many questions to arise in the minds of readers and I will undoubtedly receive many letters of inquiry. In the last three years I have received several thousand. After a reasonable time I shall revise this volume and cover all of the important inquiries that are made hereafter. One question has been asked with such frequency in the last few days as to justify its answer now by Appendix A, which consists of a resolution, a letter (which I have selected from letters that I have received from bankers), my answer to that letter and an article from *The North American* of Philadelphia. Following this explanation, these are quoted in the order named. They are:

63D CONGRESS, 1ST SESSION.
H. RES. 80.
IN THE HOUSE OF REPRESENTATIVES.
April 29, 1913.

Mr. LINDBERGH submitted the following resolution; which was referred to the Committee on Rules and ordered to be printed.

RESOLUTION.

Whereas there is general need of legislation on banking and currency, and also a general understanding that such legislation is to be enacted soon, possibly at this extra session of Congress, but that notwithstanding that fact no Committee on Banking and Currency has been selected by the House; and

Whereas this proposed legislation on banking and currency is of great importance—exceeding in importance that of tariff or any other legislation contemplated by this Congress—and therefore should receive the most careful and impartial consideration, especially having in view the following facts:

Ever since the Civil War Congress has allowed the bankers to control financial legislation. The membership of the Finance Committee in the Senate (now the Banking and Currency Committee) and the Committee on Banking and Currency in the House have been made up chiefly of bankers, their agents, and their attorneys. These committees have controlled the nature of bills to be reported, the extent of them, and the debates that were to be held on them when they were being considered in the Senate and the House. No one not on the committee is recognized under the practice of

289

the House as long as a member on the committee wishes recognition, and one of them is sure to hold the floor unless some one favorable to the committee has been arranged for. In this way the committees have been able to control legislation in the interests of the few.

The men who have appointed the committees in the last fifty years have not had the clear and earnest viewpoint of our forefathers. On Tuesday, January fourteenth, seventeen hundred and ninety-four, the following resolution was introduced in the United States Senate:

"Nor shall any person holding any office or stock in any institution in the nature of a bank, for issuing or discounting bills or notes payable to bearer or order, under the authority of the United States, be a member of either House whilst he holds such office or stock."

It passed the Senate two days later, after being fought by the bankers, and amended at their instigation in order that they might be allowed to sit in Congress, but it still remained a protest to bankers controlling legislation in which they were personally interested.

Our finances, including the actual control of legislation in Congress, have been surrendered to the bankers, their agents, and attorneys. At the earlier date above stated, when people were less commercial and more determined to have all public acts removed from the influence of personal interest than people are now, they feared to trust the bankers, even as plain Members of Congress, to frame legislation. We of this age allow them to absolutely control all of the committees in Congress that make the laws governing financial operations. Some of the members of these committees belong to banking associations that lobby in Congress as a means of securing action favorable to the bankers.

The English money lenders have co-operated with those of our country, and in eighteen hundred and sixty-two an agent, quietly and under a sort of confidential seal, distributed among the aristocrats and the wealthy class a circular. It was called the Hazard Circular and related in a way to the Civil War. It read:

"Slavery is likely to be abolished by the war power and all chattel slavery abolished. This I and my European friends are in favor of, for slavery is but the owning of labor and carries with it the care of the laborers, while the European plan, led on by England, is that capital shall control labor by controlling wages. The great debt that the capitalists will see to it is made out of the war, must be used as a means to control the volume of money. To accomplish this the bonds must be used as a banking basis. We are now waiting for the Secretary of the Treasury to make this recommendation to Congress. It will not do to allow the greenback, as it is called, to circulate as money any length of time, as we can not control that. But we can control the bonds and through them the bank issues."

Near the close of the war, eighteen hundred and sixty-five, Mr. Jay Cooke, the fiscal agent for the Government, published a circular and in it stated, among other things:

"We lay down the proposition that our national debt made permanent and rightly managed, will be a national blessing. The funded debt of the United States is the addition of $3,000,000,000 to the previously realized wealth of the Nation. It is three thousand millions added to the actual available capital."

Again, in eighteen hundred and seventy-seven, a circular was issued by authority of the Associated Bankers of New York, Philadelphia, and Boston. It was signed by one James Buel, secretary, and sent out from two hundred and forty-seven Broadway, New York. It was sent to the bankers in all of the States. It read:

"DEAR SIR: It is advisable to do all in your power to sustain such prominent daily and weekly newspapers, especially the agricultural and religious press, as will oppose the greenback issue of paper money; and that you also withhold patronage from all applicants who are not willing to oppose the Government issue of money. Let the Government issue the coin and the banks issue the paper money of the country, for then we can better protect each other. To repeal the Act creating bank notes, or to restore to circulation the Government issue of money, will be to provide the people with money and will therefore seriously affect our individual profits as bankers and lenders. See your Congressman at once and engage him to support our interests, that we may control legislation."

Again, in eighteen hundred and ninety-three, a circular was sent out by the American Bankers' Association, an organization in which most bankers hold membership. It is known as the "Panic circular of eighteen hundred and ninety-three," bears date March eleventh, eighteen hundred and ninety-three, and was mailed to the national banks. It reads as follows:

"DEAR SIR: The interests of national banks require immediate financial legislation by Congress. Silver, silver certificates, and Treasury notes must be retired and national-bank notes upon a gold basis made the only money. This will require the authorization of five hundred millions to one thousand millions of new bonds as the basis of circulation.

You will at once retire one-third of your circulation and call in one-half of your loans. Be careful to make a monetary stringency among your patrons, especially among influential business men. Advocate an extra session of Congress to repeal the purchasing clause of the Sherman law and act with other banks of your city in securing a large petition to Congress for its unconditional repeal, per accompanying form. Use personal influence with your Congressman, and particularly let your wishes be known to your Senators. The future life of national banks, as fixed and safe investments, depends upon immediate action, as there is an increasing sentiment in favor of Government legal-tender notes and silver coinage."

At about the time of the formation of the National Monetary Commission, in nineteen hundred and eight, certain interests formed a league with branches in many of the States, all of which have since been and still are actively engaged in an attempt to influence Congress in favor of legislation in substance the same as that recommended by the National Monetary Commission, the membership of which commission was chiefly composed of bankers, their agents and their attorneys; and

Whereas because of so much personal financial interest and the influence on the part of persons with such interest it is important that the Committee on Banking and Currency should be made up from Members of Congress who have no personal financial interest in the results of the legislation to be enacted; and

Whereas the present practice of the House in the formation of its committees is to have recommendations of Members for the committees made from three certain different sources, and invariably the House pro forma elects the Members as thus recommended: Now, therefore, be it

Resolved, That it is the sense of the House that no Member should serve on the Banking and Currency Committee who is a banker, or agent or attorney of any bank or banks, or who is the owner of any bank stock or other interest in a bank, or who is directly or indirectly interested in the profits of any banking business.

The following is one of the letters that I received from bankers:

Capital and Surplus $45,000.00

J. W. Benson, Prest.   W. H. Jarmuth, Cash.
C. M. Doughty, V. Prest.   Paul Benson, Asst. Cash.

THE FIRST NATIONAL BANK
of Heron Lake,
HERON LAKE, MINNESOTA, April 30, 1913.

HON. REP. LINDBERGH,
    Washington, D. C.

DEAR SIR:—The enclosed clipping from the *St. Paul Dispatch*, in reference to your resolution regarding appointment of committee on banking and currency, explains itself. If the press is correct in stating your attitude in regard to this committee, we would suggest that we have several men in this town who would unquestionably qualify for the position; they have no direct connection with banks, do not participate in the profits of banking, are neither depositors, and very much against their will, are neither borrowers, and no doubt would consider the interests of the common people in serving on your committee.

Seriously do not believe that your theory will work out in practice, and in working out banking reform in this country, believe the advice and counsel of our best bankers is imperative.

Yours respectfully,
W. H. JARMUTH,
Cashier.

The following is my answer to Mr. Jarmuth:

HOUSE OF REPRESENTATIVES

WASHINGTON, May 5, 1913.

MR. W. H. JARMUTH,
    Cashier, First National Bank,
        Heron Lake, Minnesota.

MY DEAR MR. JARMUTH :—

Replying to your letter enclosing article from *St. Paul Dispatch*, commenting on my resolution, you will notice from the resolution itself, a copy of which I inclose, that you can get a better understanding by reading it in connection with the article.

My interest in this subject is that of a citizen together with the additional responsibility of now representing the people as one of their many officials. Many bankers and other people from all of the States have written me very many letters on the subject of banking and currency. Some have expressed themselves from the same viewpoint that you do, but as a rule they do not take that position. Of course any of us can be mistaken, and I shall at all times be ready to correct any mistake that I may make. Therefore I am glad to receive these letters. You have not, however, convinced me that I am mistaken about the propriety of the passage of my resolution by Congress.

Of course it is not a matter of concern to the public what your and my personal affairs and those of the persons to whom you refer in your letter are. As for myself, no banker has ever refused to make me loans on my personal notes without security. The bankers generally know that my activity in these matters of banking and currency is not a personal affront to them. I am simply doing what I believe to be my duty as an official and I number among my best friends many bankers. I have no prejudice in the matter.

As to the unnamed persons to whom you refer, not knowing them, of course I cannot express an opinion about their fitness, but I think people generally would agree with me in my belief that there are many citizens in your community as well as in all other communities whom it would be wiser for the public generally to have determine what laws and rules should govern the banking and currency business than to have you do it. I do not make that statement as a reflection upon either your ability or your absolute honesty and integrity, but because I believe that all persons sitting in judgment on any matter should not have a personal financial interest other than that of citizens in general. I have observed that most people are influenced by their personal interest. History proves that to have always been so.

You know that no juror or judge would be allowed to sit in trial on a case who had a personal financial interest in the decision to be given. I know that the bankers have a personal financial interest in the banking and currency laws that are to be enacted. They should not be allowed to decide what those laws are to be. But of course, it is their privilege and right to appear before an impartial committee and give advice and testimony. Every interest should have representatives before the committee who would give information, but the committee should be the representative of the general public, which includes all of the people in all kinds of business as well as those who are not in business. That is necessary in order to have general consistency, so that all may be on an equality in the enactment and administration of the law.

On the same day I received your letter, it happened that an editorial which is germane to this subject, appeared in the *Washington Herald*, D. C. I quote a few sentences from it:

"SECRETARY McADOO AND THE BANKS.

"The new Secretary of the Treasury has interfered with one of the long standing privileges of the national banks in requiring them to pay 2 per cent interest on deposits of the national funds.

"From the day of the foundation of the national banks they have had the free use of these funds and have, as a result, profited many millions out of the transaction. * * * Now, when it comes down to proper business methods and requirements, it is very difficult to understand why the banks should not be obliged to pay over to the Federal Treasury all of the profits they are making continually out of Uncle Sam's funds intrusted to their care, and incidentally strengthening their ready cash assets, whenever pushed for currency.

"It is the nature of man to acquire all the privileges that come his way. To paraphrase a well-known quotation on 'greatness'; 'Some are born privileged, some acquire privilege, and some have privilege thrust upon them.' Our national banks have had privilege thrust upon them. The whole scheme was so cleverly devised and applied that it was many years before even well-informed men had any idea of the 'cinch' hold which these institutions had secured upon the business and finances of the country. The government is back of them. It supplies them with all the currency they require free of charge and, besides, pays them interest on the securities upon which their note circulation is based. Come to look at this with closer scrutiny it must be admitted that the protection granted certain lines of industry and manufacture by the tariff is a mild thing when compared with that which the Federal Government spreads over the national banks."

In order that you may see further that it is no fancy in my mind that caused me to introduce the resolution, I am enclosing you an article from the *North American* of Philadelphia, which comments on the resolution.

Trusting that with these explanations you will understand that this work on my part is fully justified by existing conditions, I am,

Sincerely yours,

C. A. LINDBERGH.

The following are comments of *The North American* of Philadelphia on my resolution:

The North American,

PHILADELPHIA, Wednesday, April 30, 1913.

WOULD EXCLUDE BANKERS FROM FRAMING MONEY BILL

REPRESENTATIVE LINDBERGH TO FIGHT TO KEEP THEM OFF HOUSE COMMITTEE—QUOTES FROM HISTORY TO SHOW DANGER.

By ANGUS McSWEEN.

WASHINGTON, April 29.

Exclusive of bankers or the representatives of banking interests from membership in the Banking and Currency Committee, as a step to prevent the bankers from further controlling legislation relating to banking and currency, is the purpose of a resolution introduced in the House today by Representative Lindbergh, of Minnesota.

Mr. Lindbergh is an independent Republican who has declared his intention of co-operating with the Progressives. He introduced the first resolution calling for an investigation of the money trust, and more than any other man in Congress forced that investigation.

It is largely as the result of the money trust investigation and the disclosures made of money and business monopolization by a combination of New York bankers that Mr. Lindbergh has offered his resolution.

The reasons he gives are set forth in a preamble of important bearing upon the whole question of banking reform now engaging the attention of the President and his advisers.

Mr. Lindbergh declares in his resolution that all banking and currency legislation since the Civil War has been controlled by the bankers of the country.

CONTROLLED CONGRESS COMMITTEES

He charges that they have controlled the Finance Committee of the Senate and the Banking and Currency Committee of the House. Not only have they directed the shaping of legislation in these committees of direct advantage to themselves, but as members of the committees they have had charge of steering the measures framed by themselves through the two houses.

He cites three tremendously important instances in the

history of the country since the Civil War, in which the bankers themselves have shown interests and views diametrically opposed to those of the general public.

The first of these was when Jay Cooke attempted to impose the bankers' view of the public debt upon the public in a circular in which he declared that the debt was a public blessing, "making an addition of three billions to the wealth of the nation in the form of three billion of actual available capital."

He quotes a circular issued by the bankers of New York, Philadelphia and Boston to the bankers of the country in 1877, in which they say:

"To restore to circulation the Government issue of money will be to provide the people with money and will therefore seriously affect our individual profits as bankers and lenders.

"See your Congressman at once and engage him to support our interest that we may control legislation."

In 1893, Mr. Lindbergh says, the American Bankers' Association sent out a circular to bankers urging them to work for the repeal of the silver purchase act, which, the circular declared, would force an issue of bonds to the amount of at least $500,000,000 and possibly as much as $1,000,000,000 and to advocate an extra session of Congress, all of which was effected.

In this circular the Bankers' Association says to its members.

"Be careful to make a monetary stringency among your patrons, especially among influential business men."

BANKERS RULED ALDRICH COMMISSION

Mr. Lindbergh declares that the Aldrich Monetary Commission was composed of bankers or the representatives of great banking interests, and that the Aldrich banking and money plan put forth by that commission was solely in the interest of the bankers.

He charges that for the purpose of promoting the Aldrich plan there was organized an association by the bankers the members of which are still working in the interest of that scheme solely for the benefit of the bankers and in opposition to the interests of the general public.

In view of all these circumstances, and the fact that it is now proposed that there shall be framed a bill to reform the banking system, Mr. Lindbergh concludes that the credit of the Congress and of the bankers themselves requires that the committee to frame the proposed legislation shall be composed of men who can have no direct financial interest in the result of such legislation.

TO PUT HOUSE ON RECORD

Mr. Lindbergh intends to demand consideration for his resolution, if possible, before the Banking and Currency Committee is appointed, and he expects to put the House on record respecting his proposition.

It will be urged upon the Democrats that since the country has now reached a point in its development where it is understood that the beneficiaries of a tariff law should not be permitted to write the tariff schedules, the application of exactly the same principle to the framing of legislation affecting banking interests makes it a monstrous impropriety to permit the bankers to write the law regulating themselves.

With his resolution and the strong arguments that can be advanced in its support, Mr. Lindbergh also raises the very important question of the right of the bankers to continue in control of the nation's credit system.

The two questions are so nearly merged that they should be considered as one, for control of legislation by bankers necessarily means the continued control of credit by the bankers, whereas if the bankers' influence in legislation can be reduced, there is a chance that President Wilson's promise to make credit free can be realized.

The present situation is already causing fear that the President may not have given as much thought to the matter of credit control as the subject deserves and that men close to the administration are seeking to involve him in a scheme of proposed legislation for the benefit of the bankers.

One reason for this fear is that men out of Congress, but in close touch with great banking interests, appear to know more about the Democratic program for banking and currency reform than do the Democratic Congressional leaders.

APPENDIX B.

I insert "Appendix B" because many people have requested me to do so. It consists of quotations taken from my arguments made before the Rules Committee for the purpose of securing the appointment of a special committee to investigate the Money Trust. I have also inserted some of my remarks on the same subject which were made before the House when the same subject was up for its consideration. I do not insert my remarks in full, because that would make this volume more bulky than I wish it to be, and it would also delay its issue somewhat. The matter inserted may not be as connected as the reader might wish, but under the circumstances I cannot avoid that. The reader will, however, be able to determine from the context which inserts were delivered before the House and which before the Rules Committee. They are as follows:

Mr. Lindbergh said:—

Mr. Speaker, it is difficult for those who have given the amount of time to the study of the Money Trust problem that it justifies to be able to understand how serious-minded men can temporize in the way that many of the Members have done in this particular case. To allow personalities or politics to influence one's action is an indication that the importance has escaped such persons as do. I do not believe that there is a Member who would neglect his duty in this particular matter if he really comprehended the situation. The only thing that I would feel like criticizing the majority membership for is the way in which it seeks to deceive the public by having time to waste on unimportant and transient matters, but when real momentous problems are up for consideration the "previous question" is ordered and Members prevented from explaining important measures. Not since the Emancipation Proclamation has so important a subject as this Money Trust been before the people for their consideration, but it is slighted by the leaders by their calling to their aid those who believe that it is more important for them to work to stand in well with the special interests than it is for them to endeavor to promote the general welfare of all of the people, and as a result having the House set aside days for the discussion of political differences and personalities, while the discussions on this important matter are limited to 5 and 12 minutes, with all discussion to be dropped at the end of two hours.

299

The Emancipation Proclamation freed 4,000,000 slaves. A proper treatment of the Money Trust resolution would emancipate over 90,000,000 industrial slaves, and yet the Money Trust investigation is treated with kindergarten methods.

There is unrest in this country. If I alone were to expose, and give emphasis in adequate terms, to the actual feeling of the people, I might be called a radical, but it does not occur to anyone to apply such terms to Judge Gary, President of the great Steel Trust. Let me quote from some remarks he made on February 14th, 1912, at the New York Lehigh Club, the following:

> "Unless capitalists, corporations, rich men, powerful men, themselves take a leading part in trying to improve conditions of humanity, great changes will come. They will come mighty quickly, and the mob will bring them."

Judge Gary made it very evident that the people generally are "evincing a readiness to take things into their own hands." He also stated that the "spirit of unrest" is not confined to the United States, but is world-wide. "Things are being said," he declared, "very similar to things said just before the French Revolution. I tell you the spark may yet make a flame, and that soon. I have an especial reason for saying this and a reason that affects you and me. Men of great power and influence in the forces of the country have not all of them done the fair thing."

Judge Gary thinks the unrest referred to to be of so serious a nature that it threatens revolution. No honest student doubts the seriousness of the unrest, nor does he doubt that there is a real cause for it. The cause is supplied by the Money Trust, and its allied interests, but in the face of its supreme importance we, here in this House, are kept from giving the matter the proper consideration because of petty politics and personalities.

I share Judge Gary's views that there is "unrest." We all know that there is unrest. But those of us who have had the time and desire to study the actual conditions and search for a remedy, know that a revolution is not the remedy. We do not believe in violence, and while there may at times be an excuse for violence, it is never justified. There are no conditions now that should lead to violence, but there are conditions that should enlist a more serious consideration of this Money Trust problem, and the economic problems, than the House gives to them. The failure of the Members to take a sufficiently statesmanlike view of the existing conditions might even furnish the cause for the very thing that Judge

Gary fears. It was a similar indifference that caused the French Revolution, and even a revolution would be better than decay.

It is indeed a misfortune that the best opportunity that has been presented to Congress in a half century for the meeting of a great common demand has, to a certain extent, had politics injected into it. To accomplish all of the good of which it is capable no politics should have been allowed to enter into the consideration. It is of the most vital importance to this country at this time that the public in general should understand the meaning of the manner in which its own finances are manipulated by the great financiers. That understanding could be secured by the appointment of a special committee, selected with a view to their fitness for making an investigation and the importance of using the information obtained in such a manner as to create the least disturbance, for it is already known that business methods have been adopted by the financial kings that are not consistent with the interests of the plain producers and consumers. There can be no justification for using facts that might be obtained as a result of the investigation for any other purpose than for the correction of the present evils. They should not be used for political purposes, but simply to bring about justice in a consistent and orderly way.

When the subject was first approached Wall Streeters saw that the resolution was loaded with powder and lead, and that it would reach to the very heart of their practices. There was an attempt to smother it, and so prevent the public from realizing its importance.

I was astounded a few weeks ago to have an emissary of Wall Street call upon me and direct my attention to the fact that I was taking an immense responsibility upon myself by pressing such a resolution for consideration, and that if I continued a panic would be brought on which would be worse than any this country had previously known. He admonished me to withdraw the resolution. To this I suggested that if there was a condition existing among the greater business interests of this country that was so rotten that an investigation revealing those conditions would cause a panic, then it was better that those conditions should be known now, in order that the future of the country might be assured at least. It is not possible to come to any conclusion other than that if the business is being dishonestly conducted, then it is necessary that an investigation should be made in order that we may learn how to correct it. How is it possible that any honest, patriotic citizen should consent to stop an investigation and thereby conceal such conditions as those intimated by the Wall Street emissary?

The Rules Committee continued to hold its hearings. It was sought to influence its chairman and members, but they refused to allow politics to enter. When that method did not succeed the next step was to threaten some of the leaders of the House with a panic before election, unless the investigation should be prevented, but in the meantime the public was making such demand that it became dangerous to the political interests to do otherwise than to at least give the appearance of making an investigation. The members of the Banking and Currency Committee were secured to conjure up in their minds a jealousy, lest their privileges should be invaded, and to demand that they should be given the privilege of making the investigation.

As long as these investigations were upon matters that did not vitally concern the special interests, the members of the committees were not so jealous of their privileges, and the less important investigations were therefore referred to special committees without the least compunction. This method for the evasion of responsibility by the representatives of the people is one of the mockeries of representative government. Wall Streeters simply entered Washington and scared the politicians into subservience. It is a matter of common knowledge among many of the Members that its emissaries have been here lobbying in opposition to this investigation. Finally, it was seen that the public demand was so great that the investigation had to come and since it was too late to have it absolutely muffled, the only thing for them to do was to refer it to a standing committee.

Now that the public is being heard from, there is some chance of awakening the standing committee to its responsibility, and force it to act with diligence.

I do not impugn the honesty of the membership of the Banking and Currency Committee, but in view of the apparent wrongs in our present system, openly demonstrated, I do, and the country must naturally, feel that the members of that committee are not over-diligent, nor even diligent, in discharging the great duty that rests upon them. They have the ability if they will apply it, but the nature of the education of most of the members of the committee has taught them to permit the very things of which the public complains.

The chairman of the committee has proposed, and there is now before us for consideration, his resolution, instead of the ones introduced by me in July and December, 1911, and on January 3rd, 1912, and one introduced by the gentleman from Texas (Mr. Henry) on January 29th, 1912. The resolutions introduced by Mr. Henry and myself would have permitted a committee to go to the bottom of the subject and treat this important matter with the respect it merits. The substance of my resolution and the one Mr. Henry introduced is the same.

The very absurdity of the phraseology of the Pujo resolution stamps upon those who are responsible for it a weakness that ought never to be shown in this House. The lack of force on the part of those composing the membership of the Banking and Currency Committee, which has charge of the investigation, is suggested in the resolution proposed by its chairman.

On June 30th, 1908, a law was passed directing the appointment of the National Monetary Commission, and that committee was appointed and authorized by law to make a thorough investigation of this problem. Mr. Pujo was one of the members of the commission. He signed its report. There is in the report a proposed bill,—the Aldrich Plan. He stands committed in its favor by having signed the report. By Section 56 of that bill it is proposed the Government of the United States shall give, absolutely free, to the proposed association approximately $220,000,000.

That is not all. In that same bill it is provided by other sections that the association may issue any amount of its notes without paying any tax whatever if the amount issued is covered by lawful money held by it. There are provisions in the bill by which the United States is to turn over its general funds, and still other provisions by which the association can secure the reserves of the banks throughout the country. These reserves which the association secures from the banks and the Government deposits will at one and the same time act as reserves for the banks and as lawful money to cover association note issues to save it from taxes. Within one year after the association would begin business it would have from the Government, and as reserve agent for the banks, lawful money on which it could, if it chose, issue more than a billion dollars to lend to its subscribing banks—a gift, pure and simple, to the great moneyed interests. Why not, if such a gift is to be made, let the people have the advantage instead of the association?

That, with almost innumerable other special privileges, was the report signed by Mr. Pujo. The gentleman, no doubt, is sincere, but he has not entered into a study of these problems in such a manner or to be able to promote the general welfare as a result of his work. He has been willing to and has signed the report by which the people of this country would grant to a private monopoly, the privilege of issuing money, free of charge, and giving it legal tender. Several other of the members of the Banking and Currency Commit-

tee served on the National Monetary Commission and signed
the same report. Are we going to turn over the investigation
of the Money Trust to be made by them? If we do, we must
expect it to be conducted from the viewpoint and in the
interests of the bankers, so far as they dare to, whereas it
is the wish of the country that it should be made for the
good of all business, and of the people in general.

The purpose of this investigation was to get such information as would enable Congress to pass proper laws on the
subject of banking and currency. We are asked to turn the
whole matter over to the bankers and the attorneys of
bankers. We would be acting according to the same principle if we were to appoint J. Pierpont Morgan, John D.
Rockefeller and Andrew Carnegie, and a few more of the
same school, to investigate the trust problems and report
their investigations and recommendations to Congress.

CONTROL OF MONEY AND CREDITS.

COMMITTEE ON RULES,
HOUSE OF REPRESENTATIVES,
Friday, December 15, 1911.

The committee met at 10:30 o'clock a. m., Hon. Robert L.
Henry (chairman) presiding.

The CHAIRMAN. Gentlemen, the committee has been called
to hear Mr. Lindbergh in reference to House resolution 314,
in regard to the Money Trust. If you are ready, Mr. Lindbergh, you may proceed.

Mr. LINDBERGH. Of course, I expect the committee, or any
of its members, to ask any questions they see fit as I proceed.
There are some parts of my brief that I shall pass over
because, as you already have copies, it will save time if I
pass along to the most material parts.

I have assumed and I believe that there is very little doubt
among those who have studied the subject closely that there
is a Money Trust, but that its form and the nature of its
operations are not generally understood.

Credits and debits, balanced by a small fraction of honest
money, might be used as an equitable measure by which producers could be paid and consumers charged for the products
and services of commerce. Unfortunately, however, a few
speculators have wedged in between the producers and consumers, and they operate and now principally control the
system of credits and debits, and through it enough of the
money so that they control the commodities by paying the
producers the least and charging the consumers the highest
price they can stand. Under that arrangement present prop-

erty and financial management conflicts with human rights and hinder general success.

Our financial system is a false one and a huge burden on the people. The money kings know that the people are bending under it, and since there are some rather loose points about it, the money kings wish, through the medium of a demand made by the people to secure a change, to manage it in the interest of Wall Street. They have proposed the Aldrich plan.

I have alleged that there is a Money Trust. The proposed Aldrich plan is a scheme plainly in the interest of the trust. There is a Money Trust, but it is not in the form of the steel, the oil, the tobacco, the railway, and the other common trusts. It is maintained and governed by an entirely different method. It is father of the others, but unlike. The Government prosecutes other trusts, and it specifically and systematically supports the Money and Credit Trust. The Government creates by indirection what it seeks to destroy by direction.

The district I represent is agricultural, and its bankers are mostly conservative and free from speculation. But, notwithstanding, they have had to follow the law of necessity created by our banking system. And to show what I mean by that statement I shall insert in my remarks three letters from banks as examples of the units from which the Money Trust gets its support, and that though the banks do not intend or desire to support the trust:

LETTER No. 1.
(Capital, $50,000.)
GERMAN-AMERICAN NATIONAL BANK,
Little Falls, Minn., November 17, 1911.
Hon. C. A. LINDBERGH,
    House of Representatives, Washington, D. C.

DEAR SIR: Replying to your letter of the 11th instant, asking some facts regarding our loans, in our report to the comptroller, under date of June 7, 1911, we reported:

	June 7, 1911.	Sept. 1, 1911.
Loans and discounts	$401,643	$421,679
Lawful money reserve	44,090	39,420
With approved reserve agents	103,020	48,208
Other national banks	2,154	643

Of the $400,000 loans, $300,000 is an average amount of outside paper, commonly known as commercial paper, and $100,000 is local paper. We have never been able to loan more than this locally for commercial purposes, but we could put out, say, $100,000 to $200,000 on good real-estate loans—farm loans—if we were permitted.

We have at present over $100,000 in savings deposits and $275,000 in time deposits in this bank, which amounts do not fluctuate very much from month to month the year round, and in my opinion 50 per cent of this could be safely invested in farm loans and be a great benefit to this county at large, and neighboring counties also.

In a recent report to the comptroller we recommended that national banks be permitted to use 25 per cent of commercial deposits and 50 per cent of time deposits for farm loans.

In times of panic it is almost impossible to realize quickly on commercial paper, especially the large amounts, but a good farm loan can always be disposed of either for cash or in exchange for credit. A bank holding good farm loans could, in case of a panic, turn over any of them to depositors in lieu of cash wanted and the party who receives it would be perfectly satisfied provided he knew there was good land back of it. I have heard of several instances of this being done, and I myself have heard people give excuses for taking out money in the bank in times of panic "to buy land where it is safe."

We therefore are very much in favor of a law permitting national banks to loan on farm property, and you are at liberty to use this letter in any way you see fit to further this end.

Yours, respectfully,

E. J. RICHIE, *Cashier*,
JOHN WETZEL, *Vice President*.

I saw published for the same bank a statement, and the amount due from approved reserve agents to that bank on December 5 was $103,171.04. That fact applying to that and all other banks is an important consideration in connection with this whole question, because I expect to show that it is the reserves that accumulate as a result of this banking system that give the Money Trust the control of the finances of this country, and the secret of their control rests principally in that the most of the reserves and a large part of the deposits are kept in the big banks that the trust controls. You will notice by the bank's statement in letter No. 1 that they have loaned out in the community from which they receive their deposits about $100,000; they have loaned out to parties who are non-residents, and live in distant places, and with whom they have no direct business, about $300,000; or, in other words, three-fourths of the deposits in that bank. There is another item about which the public in general knows little, namely, that these country banks are obliged to take the deposits that are placed with them by the people who reside in the community in which they are doing business, and loan them to distant borrowers, which results in the money being of no service to the community in which it was presumably earned.

Mr. GARRETT. Why is that? Why are they compelled to do that?

Mr. LINDBERGH. Because our national banking laws, and our banking laws in general, do not give the country banks an opportunity to invest in those enterprises that are going on in their own midst. They can not loan to a farmer because farmers usually require long-time loans, and yet those banks are taking time deposits. The time deposits of this bank referred to in letter No. 1 amount, I believe, to about $300,000. That bank should be given the opportunity of loaning on securities part of its deposits which are made on time. The deposits which are there for checking in the usual way should be liquid, liquid all the time, so as to carry on the commerce of the country. There is a distinction between the two that we shall have to keep in mind.

Mr. LENROOT. Are not time deposits subject to call at any time?

Mr. LINDBERGH. They are subject to call in general because if a bank refuse to pay a time deposit its credit would suffer.

Mr. FOSTER. The same as any other deposits; and they simply lose the interest; that is all.

Mr. LINDBERGH. Yes; they simply lose the interest in practice.

Mr. WILSON. Is there any bank that, if all the depositors made a demand for their deposits at the same time, could pay up?

Mr. LINDBERGH. There is not. It would be a bad bank for the community to keep its condition such that it could pay up instantly, unless it got help from the outside.

Mr. WILSON. I know; but they have only received the deposit, have they not, of these particular depositors?

Mr. LINDBERGH. Yes. They received them to be handled in the usual safe way. A bank that would receive deposits and leave them in the vaults would be a detriment to the community in which it did business.

Mr. WILSON. There is no question about that.

Mr. FOSTER. You understand that these foreign loans you

speak of are many times commercial paper, sent out by large corporations that float paper at certain times. Is that what you mean by that—foreign loans?

Mr. LINDBERGH. Yes, that is what I mean by foreign loans.

Mr. FOSTER. You speak, for instance, of farmers. Is it your idea, then, that there ought to be a change in the national banking law permitting them to loan on long-time paper?

Mr. LINDBERGH. Yes, a certain amount of their time deposits.

Mr. FOSTER. How long a time?

Mr. LINDBERGH. At least a year.

Mr. DENVER. Do you mean that they should be allowed to take mortgage loans?

Mr. LINDBERGH. Mortgage loans. Of course, the time is a mere matter of detail. I would not have it drawn for too long a time, understand.

Mr. FOSTER. What is your idea, that the amount of loans they could make is to be governed not in limited amount?

Mr. LINDBERGH. In that way? Yes; limited to a certain per cent of their deposits.

Mr. FOSTER. Yes.

Mr. LINDBERGH. There should be a limit to it, such as experience shows would be safe. I have letters from probably 100 bankers, and they to a unit agree that it would be better for the banking business, and better for the communities in which they are doing business, if they were permitted to use a certain per cent of time deposits to make loans on securities and for reasonable length of time on farms.

Mr. FOSTER. You confuse time deposits there, I think, because they are all deposits subject to call.

Mr. LINDBERGH. I understand; but the practical effect is time, and it is its practical effect that I consider in these matters.

Mr. FOSTER. They are all subject to be withdrawn at any time.

Mr. LINDBERGH. They are all subject to be withdrawn at any time, and this bank letter No. 1 that I have in the notes particularly defines the conditions with reference to those. The bankers generally, who have written to me, say that they can convert their mortgage loans into cash quicker than they can convert the commercial paper; and that is my experience, too, in what I have observed. I have observed the operation of that business to a considerable extent. Depositors not needing to use their money would be glad in times of panics to get safely secured paper.

Mr. LENROOT. The claim has been made a great many times that independent organizations have been able to do business independently only because of the opportunity to float their commercial loans through these banks outside of the great money centers; that if it was not for them the trusts and combinations, the New York financiers, would be able to bring them to time. I would like to hear what you have to say on that.

Mr. LINDBERGH. The first consideration of a bank, in the beginning of its business and throughout its continuance, should be to take care of the community from which it receives its deposits. I do not think anybody will question that. The people who are there doing business, whether it is farming or what-not, should be taken care of by the natural business of that community. I think the banks should have the right, when they have taken care of their local demands, to go outside and buy commercial paper. I do not question that, and I think there is big force in the point that Mr. Lenroot makes, and they should have the opportunity when the circumstances of their own localities favor it or justify the investment of deposits in other localities.

All the banks that reported to me desire the privilege of loaning on real estate, and firmly believe that proper real-estate loans can be realized on more readily and are better in times of panic than commercial paper, and decidedly better than that taken from speculators and others from the cities.

It is well to bear in mind a distinction between money that is used as property, that is, a commodity, and money used as an agent of exchange. Money used as a commodity, like that deposited by wage earners, farmers, professional men, and others, who do not use the deposits in commercial transactions, should be treated in a different way in regard to its investment than commercial deposits that are subject to check in the ordinary way. The true purpose of money is its commercial use and all notes and accounts used in commerce should be liquid and kept so at all times. The deposits made on time certificates should be loaned principally on securities, while deposits subject to the ordinary checking system, for commercial purposes, should only be loaned on short-time commercial paper. The accounts of the two classes of deposits should be separated in so far as it is practical. Notice the statement in letter No. 1. You will see that the savings deposits and time certificates combined are a little in excess of paper held by the bank against makers from other localities. The deposits used to carry the $300,000 paper taken from remote districts should be loaned to farmers and others in the locality where the deposits originate. That would also give confidence to the savings and time depositors. The bank making that statement shows that the officers fully

appreciate the justice of responding to the legitimate demands
of the locality from which it gets deposits, and that is true
of all banks doing business independent of the Money Trust.

I commend for the study of Members letter No. 1 as giving
a true state of conditions in the country districts. The other
letters are as good on the facts they cover, and the study of
the three is the A, B, C on which we can, in one respect, base
an amendment to the banking laws that will save the country
districts especially from some of the evil effects of panics,
and it would lessen speculation in the cities.

The deposits of banks in other banks—that is, with each
other—is the first start for the Money Trust.

Probably no banker in my district has the slightest idea
that he furnishes the seed from which the Money Trust has
grown, but I shall prove that they and their fellow-bankers
there and elsewhere are doing that very thing.

The CHAIRMAN. On that point, then, you do not contend
that the bankers throughout the country in the respective
States, and the bankers in these money centers, are in agreement, and have organized a Money Trust?

Mr. LINDBERGH. No; they have not. There are as many
honest men among the bankers as there are in any other
business.

The CHAIRMAN. In other words, you do not think there is
any conspiracy.

Mr. LINDBERGH. I do not think there is a conspiracy on
the part of the banks in general. I believe that a few banks
in New York form the backbone of the real Money Trust.

The CHAIRMAN. I understand. I mean in general.

Mr. LINDBERGH. Oh, no; not in the least can the bankers
in general be charged with deliberately maintaining a Money
Trust.

Deposits are substantially the assets of the banks. They
term them liabilities, but it is from these principally that the
bankers make their loans and also their profits. The
accounts are due to the depositors, but the banks use the
deposits for making loans. Consistently, the most of them
prefer to loan in the locality from which they get their
deposits. That would bring local repetition of deposits.

Bankers generally are fair and accommodating in their
business, as that business is conducted. But the banking laws
make it impracticable for them to loan all of their deposits
in the localities of their origin. It can be done in large cities,
where the money kings, gamblers, and speculators reside (all
of whom are heavy borrowers from the banks and take all
that they can get).

Mr. LENROOT. Right there, for information. Are what are

termed as commercial loans loans of this character, commercial paper by stock gamblers, and so on?

Mr. LINDBERGH. The country banks figure all short-time paper that they buy as commercial paper.

Mr. LENROOT. I mean, as a matter of practice, are they that character of paper, or are they the paper of the large business houses, like Wanamaker and Marshall Field?

Mr. LINDBERGH. That is the real, true commercial paper.

Mr. LENROOT. What is the fact? That is what I am asking for.

Mr. LINDBERGH. The fact is, they use all kinds of paper they buy as commercial paper, or short-time paper.

Mr. LENROOT. I mean, what do they buy? What is the character of the paper they do actually buy?

Mr. LINDBERGH. They actually buy paper of the character of Wanamaker & Co. and other companies like that. A large part of the paper is made by companies of that character. But they get paper that is made by speculators, men of means, you know, who buy for a rise in the market. They are satisfied if they get good paper.

Mr. GARRETT. In regard to reserves, your country bank is required to retain 15 per cent?

Mr. LINDBERGH. Six per cent in its vaults.

Mr. GARRETT. Six per cent in its vaults and 9 per cent of it they put in a reserve. Then the bank in which it places that reserve is required to retain only 25 per cent of that 9 per cent?

Mr. LINDBERGH. And if it is a reserve bank it may redeposit it in another reserve or central reserve bank.

Mr. GARRETT. And so on; so that eventually it really works out to where there is almost only the 6 per cent that is really held?

Mr. LINDBERGH. Not very much more; not any more in the bank of original deposit. Certainly not. Farmers and wage earners can borrow but little from the banks, and especially from national banks, because they are not allowed to loan on real estate nor make long-time loans. Some of the national banks in the country violate the law and do make loans on real estate. They can better justify that than the New York banks can justify their continuous violation of the banking laws in other respects.

Another practice of most banks outside of the speculative centers and of which little is known by the public or depositors is the buying of notes from brokers. These are the notes of speculators and others in the large centers, and this is another form of diverting moneys from the country to the speculating and banking centers. There is no record of the sums so diverted. The bank statements include these in the item, "Loans and discounts," which item covers all loans, and there is no way to separate them. The notes, as a rule, are purchased by the banks that carry large deposits in reserve bank cities. It is simply an additional way of employing the deposits that can not be used in the locality of their origin because the banking laws are made for Wall Street. Bankers are not to blame for this. It is simply a condition to which they are compelled to adjust, and the amount of the funds thus diverted from the channels of their origin is a large one.

It will be seen in letter No. 1 that this small country bank alone loaned $300,000 to parties outside of its banking district. Most country banks have such loans. In my home county, covered by letter No. 1, there is now and has been at all times a demand within the county by borrowers who had first-class security to give, for more than the amount of all the bank deposits in the county. These borrowers secure their loans through local agents, who charge them a commission for getting money from mortgage companies and individuals in other and usually distant places.

The farmers, wage earners, and others who save and deposit money in the local banks would be benefited if their money were loaned in the localities in which they live, and the borrowers would secure the same at less cost, but "No" has to be said to them, because, under our banking laws, speculators are given the preference. There is no objection to banks making safe loans in localities other than that in which they do business, when the local demands are not sufficient for safe loans. But the law should not obstruct loaning in a way most natural and desirable to those needing to borrow in the localities where deposits originate. That would encourage local enterprise, be a saving in addition, and a mutual advantage to bankers and borrowers, and not a breeder of panics.

If banks were permitted to accommodate the community in which they do business it would make a home outlet for their deposits, and then the payment of interest by banks to other banks could be prohibited, for that would make it practicable to reduce the deposits of banks with each other to the amount required for exchange purposes. It would remove some elements of danger in panics and reduce the power of the Money Trust. An act to accomplish that should postpone the taking effect until there could be a natural adjustment.

Mr. Foster. You treat that as if they are loaning as speculators?

Mr. Lindbergh. To speculators.

Mr. Foster. That most banks are speculative centers. As

was said by Mr. Lenroot, these commercial houses handle paper—that is, their brokers—and send out these notes, or a description of them, and the banks buy them, as I understand?

Mr. LINDBERGH. Yes, sir,

Mr. FOSTER. You do not treat them as speculative notes, do you?

Mr. LINDBERGH. Sometimes they are; not as a general rule. There is another class of loans that banks make in which I include the term "broker." For instance, a good many of the banks in Minnesota loan to parties in Dakota, or some other State, through other banks out there. I consider those bankers, through whom they get such paper, when they act in that respect, as brokers.

Mr. DENVER. Is that for the purpose of stock speculation?

Mr. LINDBERGH. Oh, no; it is not.

Mr. FOSTER. They are not speculators?

Mr. LINDBERGH. No; they are not speculators in the sense of bonding stocks.

Mr. LENROOT. Do you think, Mr. Lindbergh, there is any substantial percentage of loans made by banks on speculators' paper?

Mr. LINDBERGH. Yes; there is.

Mr. LENROOT. I mean made direct by the banks?

Mr. LINDBERGH. Not a large per cent of their deposits are made direct to speculators, except in the large cities.

Mr. LENROOT. But a large percentage of what are known as commercial loans?

Mr. LINDBERGH. Yes; there is a considerable per cent of that.

Mr. LENROOT. It would not be considered very safe banking, would it, in any community where a bank did that?

Mr. LINDBERGH. Perhaps I should give an explanation there. I consider a person who is buying a large quantity of timber out in Oregon, or any other State, a speculator in that timber. I do not mean that I confine the term "speculator" to persons who deal in bonds and stocks, but any person who uses the money that he obtains to invest in property on which he expects to receive a profit by a resale of it is a speculator.

Mr. LENROOT. Through its raising value?

Mr. LINDBERGH. Yes. He is a speculator.

Mr. WILSON. Then you would consider a man trying to corner the wheat market a speculator?

Mr. LINDBERGH. I certainly would.

Mr. LENROOT. Most anybody would.

Mr. WILSON. Is it not true there in Chicago that the board of trade men borrow great sums of money from the Chicago banks on their notes?

Mr. LENROOT. I think they put up collateral for everything they get.

Mr. LINDBERGH. Most of those people put up collateral.

Mr. WILSON. Not all of them. I think the character of the man has a great deal to do with that. I think many of the men there can borrow great sums of money.

Mr. LINDBERGH. The creation of the National Monetary Commission was a very clever move.

It was in 1907 that nature had responded so beautifully to the farmer's touch and gave this country the most bountiful crop it ever had. Other industries were busy, too, and from a natural standpoint all the conditions were right for a most prosperous year.

If the Government and business had been properly managed, the resulting condition should have been one of happiness and prosperity, and it would have been a year to make us all happy. Instead, a panic entailed enormous losses on us. Not many of us knew the cause. Wall Street was wise, and it knew that we were demanding a remedy against a recurrence of such a ridiculously unnatural condition.

Most of the Senators and Members then fell into Wall Street's trap and passed the Aldrich-Vreeland emergency-currency bill. Its ostensible purpose was to provide an emergency currency, but the real purpose was to get a monetary commission which would ultimately frame a proposition for amendments to our currency and banking laws which would suit the Money Trust.

All banks except those in control of the money kings were scared. These money kings, in so far as it seemed necessary to them, took everything in hand, including the funds of the Government. They managed that panic. The Government was helpless in their hands and did nothing except to aid them.

The New York Clearing House is an institution in the control of the Money Trust. Its certificates were issued to pay depositors instead of money. The New York banks refused to pay the country banks the reserves due them. Some of these had been deposited directly by the country banks and others indirectly through the reserve banks. The New York banks simply defied and violated the law.

If a country bank had done that, it would have been closed by a bank examiner. If a group of country banks had attempted it, they would all have been closed. But the New York Clearing House issued clearing-house certificates and forced us to accept them as money. If the United States had issued certificates to help the people in that time of stress, the Wall Street Money Trust would have vetoed it.

It would even have dared to veto such an action by the Government. But the Government did not dare to veto the New York banks' clearing-house system.

The Money Trust did other things. It intimidated some of the country banks for which it acted as reserve agent from paying cash to depositors. It ordered them to pay in clearing-house certificates. Through the guardianship of the Morgan-Rockefeller régime some of the more influential of the cities did resort to the New York Clearing House system to pay deposits.

The Money Trust at different times has sent notices to certain of its agents and those in community of interest to tighten up the money market and raise the rates of interest.

Merely as a suggestion of one of the methods, I quote from another letter such parts as seem to the point. I omit all parts that would identify the parties, for the reason that it seems best to do so if their testimony is later to be secured. The original is in my office, and it can be seen by any member of the Rules Committee. It is as follows:

NORTH DAKOTA, *July* 29, 1911.

Hon. C. A. LINDBERGH, *Washington, D. C.*

DEAR SIR: In the investigation of the Money Trust you can get valuable information from * * *.

He has a personal knowledge that the * * * was invited to join in tying up money more than a year and a half ago to raise interest rates, and the rates were raised, as you know. * * * refused to go in, but had to follow suit in raising the rates after that was accomplished. Some one should interview * * * without his knowing beforehand for what purpose, and he will give them a lead that can be followed up and which will open up a great many facts of value for the investigating committee. Of course my name must not be mentioned in any way, either publicly or to * * *, but this letter may, if you deem it proper, be shown to the committee, and afterwards you had better retain it yourself.

*   *   *   *   *   *   *

Respectfully.   ———— ————.

The first relief must be provided through the country banks. It is our duty to amend the banking laws in such a manner as will provide an outlet for their deposits without sending them into the speculative centers, where they are used to corner the staples and services needed by the people and to bring on panics. A few simple amendments to the banking laws will relieve the country bankers of the necessity of sending their depositors' money to the speculative centers. No

report from the National Monetary Commission is necessary
for that.

We need an entirely new money and banking system. But
first we must know some things concerning the financial situation that the Monetary Commission has failed to furnish.
We need some additional information, and we can then build
a permanent, honest money and banking system.

The people must know the ins and outs of the treatment
they have received at the hands of the Money Trust, in order
to avoid its pitfalls. After that they can not be bluffed out
of an honest money just because of the Money Trust
challenge.

Why does the Money Trust press so hard for the Aldrich
plan now, before the people know what the Money Trust has
been doing? Has it not got the Aldrich-Vreeland emergency
law, an act of its own concoction, that does not expire until
1914? It said, when it fooled Congress to pass that act, that
it was a sure remedy for panics. It knew we were scared
of panics then. We had just been pinched by one.

We should stand ready to pass honest money and banking
laws as soon as we can secure such facts as will safely
guide us.

I have already discussed the use that the Wall Street
Money Trust makes of the so-called depositors' "sacred
reserves." The present fixed bank reserves is the rock on
which prosperity may run at any time and produce a panic.
Prosperity ran onto that rock in 1907.

The fixed reserves are the practical holdings of the Money
Trust and they want to make them larger by the rules of the
proposed National Reserve Association, for it is provided by
that plan that all subscribing banks must conform to the
requirements in so far as reserves are to be held against
deposits of various classes, and that there shall be no change
in the percentage required by the law to be held against
demand deposits by national banks in the different localities,
and that hereafter the same percentages of reserve shall be
required of all subscribing banks—meaning the National
Reserve Association—in the same localities.

That is intended to comprehend State banks and trust companies, which under the latest Aldrich plan are eligible to sub-
scribe to the National Reserve Association.

No, the Wall Street Money Trust can not let go of the
"sacred reserves." "There shall be no change," but on the
contrary it wants to increase them by adding more banks to
follow the same rule. They always have had the use of the
reserves. They never have been used for the depositors
except after actual insolvency, and the insolvency of a bank

brings loss to depositors, so the "sacred reserves" are most sacred to the Wall Street Money Trust.

A proper investigation of the trust will show the wrong that has been perpetrated on the people by this false fixed reserve—fixed—fixed—why, of course the Money Trust wants fixed reserves so that it can absolutely depend on having them. The penalty visited on depositors, if they insist on taking them away from the trust, is insolvency of the banks that would have them to pay their depositors.

The Money Trust for many years has had practically a billion dollars of fixed reserves—"sacred reserves"—to use in speculation and to manipulate, secure corners in stocks, capture and control railways and industrial companies, and to buy and own the Nation's enterprises and its natural resources, making them vested rights in the trust, on which they may fix fabulous values on which to issue bonds and watered stocks and annually compound interest as a fixed charge on this and future generations. That is what the "sacred fixed reserves" have done for the Money Trust.

We still have with us a few veterans of the Civil War, some who fought for the emancipation of slavery and others who fought against it. On both sides there is now a common agreement that right prevailed, and personal and sectional prejudice has ceased. It is now our duty to show by our actions and appreciation of the victory that came to the Union soldiers at enormous sacrifice, that we still stand for freedom, and if we preserve it their sacrifice was not in vain. This appreciation surely is seconded by those who fought in the other battle lines in the first great struggle and they now recognize the justice of the maintenance of the principles settled in that struggle. We all join now in seeking to make those principles practical. We are of one heart and one soul, an inseparable national brotherhood, and unite in the acknowledgment of the wisdom and prophetic foresight of the immortal Abraham Lincoln when, near the close of the war, he gave utterance to the following:

"Yes; we may all congratulate ourselves that this cruel war is nearing its close. It has cost a vast amount of treasure and blood. The best blood of the flower of American youth has been freely offered upon our country's altar that the Nation might live. It has been, indeed, a trying hour for the Republic; but I see in the future a crisis approaching that unnerves me and causes me to tremble for the safety of my country. As a result of the war, corporations have been enthroned and an era of corruption in high places will follow, and the money power of the country will endeavor to prolong its reign by working upon the prejudices of the people until wealth is aggregated in a few hands and the Republic is destroyed. I feel at this moment more anxiety for the safety of my country than ever before, even in the midst of war."

NCL - p. 107

p 117.
p. 127
p 135.

p. 216, 17, 230.